COMMUNICATING to MIDDLE SCHOOLERS

"After 40 years of communicating to middle schoolers—sometimes from a stage, weekly in my small group—I'm still learning. This is partly because middle schoolers keep changing; and it's partly because . . . well . . . I still have more to learn, more to improve. Ashley's engaging and practical book both encouraged and challenged me. My biggest risk (after all these years) is getting in the rut of doing things the same way week after week after week. This book reminded me of core essentials and pushed me to experiment with approaches that are new to me."

—**Mark Oestreicher, Founder and Partner at The Youth Cartel and Author of** *Middle School Ministry*, *Understanding Your Young Teen*, **and many others**

"Ashley provides a deep dive into how to communicate to a special group of youth—middle schoolers. Her knowledge and heart for students in the middle are evident through her stories. At the end of each chapter, there are thought-provoking questions for review. The answers should lead youth workers to a working action plan to sharpen their communication skills. A must-read for middle school ministry leaders and workers!"

—**Dr. Virginia Ward, Dean of Boston Campus Gordon-Conwell Theological Seminary, co-author of** *It's Personal*, **and** *Five Views on the Future of Youth Ministry: Perspectives on What Could or Should Be*

"I can think of no one more passionate about and qualified to lead middle school aged humans, than Ashley Bohinc. With over a decade of working as a Middle School educator and pastor, Ashley knows the ever-changing needs unique to this age group as well as the unparalleled value of helping a middle schooler feel seen and inspired. This book is filled with practical insights for anyone who communicates to Middle Schoolers. Read it all and return often to the ideas and techniques she suggests. No one will appreciate it more than the middle schoolers in your ministry."

—**Kristen Ivy, President of Orange and Parent Cue, Co-author of over 24 books including** *Don't Miss It* **and** *It's Personal*

"There are few things in ministry that get me more excited, and more nervous, than speaking to middle schoolers, and that's why I'm so thankful Ashley took the time to write this book to help us out! Before I sat down to write this endorsement, I was white-boarding a junior high message and a whole bunch of Ashley's insight and wisdom influenced the way I approached it; things I wouldn't have thought about or included in the past! Read this book, take notes, and prayerfully insert some of your learnings the next time you prepare a lesson for young teens . . . you'll be glad you did!"

—Kurt Johnston, NextGen Pastor at Saddleback Church and Author of *Controlled Chaos, Making Sense of Junior High Ministry* and *How to Be the Best Volunteer Youth Worker in the History of the World*

"Few leaders know the world of middle schoolers more than Ashley Bohinc. In this new book, she drives straight to the point of what it takes to leave a lasting impression on such an important part of our future. This book is inspiring but also imminently practical, with real-life examples, suggestions for structure, and tips for handling surprises. Ashley knows these kids, and she knows how to help leaders make the best possible impact with them."

—Reggie Joiner, CEO/Founder of Orange, Author of more than 30 books including *Think Orange*, *It's Personal* and *Lead Small*

"Middle school is the new high school. Students are growing up faster now, not because they are more mature but because they are more exposed to so much so early on. Standing in the gap to translate all of this for them is you—a middle school ministry communicator. With all due respect to those of us who communicate to adults, your job is far more impactful. After all, you're impacting the future. It's why I'm so grateful to Ashley for writing this book. I've seen her impact the students in the church I started, and it's why I'm confident this book will help you and the students you serve."

—Jeff Henderson, Founding Pastor at Gwinnett Church and Author of *Know What You're For* and *What to Do Next*

"Ashley Bohinc is a prime example of leading the way in practicing what you preach. *Communicating to Middle Schoolers* gives vision on why this content matters, and it also provides practical application on how to get it done in ways that are fun and engaging. Sitting in the room with middle schoolers as Ashley was speaking at our summer camp, I experienced firsthand the laughter, 'aha' moments, and the connection to the content as our middle schoolers were soaking it all in. Every middle school speaker needs to read this book!"

—Megan Bagnall, Next Gen Core Pastor at Willow Creek Community Church

"*Communicating to Middle Schoolers* left me inspired about the opportunity to speak to young teens. After reading it, I couldn't wait to craft my next talk. This book provides everything you need to be a more effective communicator to young teens with their developmental process in mind."

—Gina Abbas, Author of *A Woman in Youth Ministry* and *Multisite Youth Ministry*

"Communicating to middle school students brings challenges and opportunities that no other age group deals with. Ashley Bohinc's knowledge and experience in speaking to middle school students are a valuable resource for any youth pastor to tap into. Ashley lays out simple and effective strategies to make your messages more memorable and more helpful to the students you are serving."

—Britt Kitchen, Student Director at North Point Ministries

"I'm so thankful Ashley wrote this book. It is jam-packed with easy-to-understand and applicable ideas and tools to take your communication with middle schoolers to the next level. With all of her expertise and experience, she is just the right person to write this book. Thanks, Ashley!"

—Rev. Dr. D.J. Coleman, Student Pastor at Northwood Church

"I knew this book would be good. But WOW, Ashley has left it all on the table. Authentic. Passionate. Inspiring. Practical. After reading this, you'll have everything—and I mean everything—you need to create a talk that will connect your message to your middle school audience. Ashley has long been a leader in this area, and she's offered every tried and tested idea to help you become an expert communicator too. If you speak to middle schoolers in any capacity, don't sleep on this one! It'll be a reference for years to come."

—Dan Scott, Author of *Caught in Between: Engage Your Preteens Before They Check Out*

Communicating to Middle Schoolers

Published by Orange, a division of The reThink Group, Inc.
5870 Charlotte Lane, Suite 300
Cumming, GA 30040 U.S.A.

The Orange logo is a registered trademark of The reThink Group, Inc.

Other Orange products are available online and direct from the publisher at thinkorange.org. Bulk copies are available at store.thinkorange.com.

ISBN: 978-1-63570-187-6

©2022 Ashley Bohinc

Writer: Ashley Bohinc

Lead Editor: Jessica Hatmaker

Editing Team: Jessica Hatmaker, Karen Wilson, Crystal Chiang, Jamal Jones, Gina Abbas, Frank DiRenzo, Ashley Johnson, Jackie Raihl, Leslie Mack, Brett Talley, Charlie Conder, Candice Wynn

Guest Contributors: Stuart Hall, Jessica Hatmaker, Jamal Jones, Charlie Conder, Jean Sohn, Vivi Diaz, Heather Flies, Katie Edwards, Mikiala Tennie, Brett Eddy, Kellen Moore, Katie Matsumoto-Moore, Gina Abbas, Stuart Makinson

Creative Director: Ashley Shugart

Cover Design: Nicole Dabbs

Book Interior Design & Layout: Ashley Shugart, Jacob Hunt

Project Management: Brian Sharp

Director of Publishing: Mike Jeffries

1 2 3 4 5 6 7 8 9 10

03/31/2022

COMMUNICATING to MIDDLE SCHOOLERS

a guide to developing and delivering messages that stick

ASHLEY BOHINC

THIS BOOK IS FOR PEOPLE WHO . . .

- ⇨ Have been asked to start teaching middle schoolers and are a little terrified.
- ⇨ Are brand-new to communicating to middle schoolers and want to learn as much as possible.
- ⇨ Know middle schoolers are important but don't know where to start.
- ⇨ Are so frustrated with middle schoolers (because they won't listen), and are desperate for anything that might work.
- ⇨ Just got asked to speak at a middle school retreat and want to up your game.
- ⇨ Are school teachers or student teachers who want to get better at speaking in a way middle schoolers understand.
- ⇨ Are leading (or hoping to one day lead) a middle school ministry and feel like they know nothing about it.
- ⇨ Have been working with middle schoolers for 20+ years and are looking to get back to the basics.
- ⇨ Are all-stars at leading a small group of middle schoolers but want to focus on growing their skills in communicating to a larger group of middle schoolers.
- ⇨ Are trying to build a teaching team for their middle school ministry and are looking for the words to help coach someone less experienced.
- ⇨ Are youth leaders responsible for both middle and high school students and naturally connect better with high schoolers but want middle schoolers to win too.

CONTENTS

FOREWORD

by Stuart Hall

Words create worlds.

When I was in middle school, my dad—a crusty, decorated Air Force Vietnam War veteran and my first coach—told me that black basketball shoes and black cleats made me look "as slow as molasses coming out of a jug in Alaska." He insisted that I wear white sneakers and cleats because they make me look faster.

And to this day, decades later, I will only wear white sneakers.

Thanks, Pops.

In eighth grade, my English teacher Mrs. Neal had our class read the classic fable "Jonathan Livingston Seagull." The rest of my classmates thought it was the dumbest book ever. Not me. A mythical story about a seagull who believes it is every seagull's right to fly left an indelible mark on my life. Richard Bach's words could not have been more timely. I felt stuck in a world where no one seemed to have goals and everyone's perspective was painfully small.

And to this day, I remember "the gull sees farthest who flies highest."

Thank you, Mrs. Neal.

Recently my wife Kellee and I visited our nation's capital. We spent one morning walking around the National Mall. Our first stop was the Dr. Martin Luther King Jr. Memorial, where we both stood in almost holy silence, spellbound. From there we walked one mile to the Lincoln Memorial, where we ascended eighty-seven steps to the chamber, then back down one flight of steps to the exact spot where Dr. Martin Luther King Jr. stood a half a century before, on August 28, 1963, and declared four words that are now etched in the stone there, circled by flowers left by visiting admirers to that hallowed spot. Four words that echo in eternity:

"I have a dream . . . "

Thank you, Dr. King.

At some point that morning in Washington D.C., Kellee and I had an epiphany: At every memorial, in every museum, inscribed in stone, displayed in lights, was a quote. Words people in the past and present had spoken. Powerful maxims. Simple principles. Epic speeches. All spoken by women and men. Ideas and truths articulated in words now stand as the foundations of a nation. And the substance of the collective of those words have created our world.

Words create worlds.

If you are holding this book and reading these words, it is safe to assume that you deeply desire the words you speak to the next generation to have that kind of lasting value. Just the opportunity to speak words of life to middle school students—who are considered by researchers to be the most anxious, digitally native, sexually fluid, multiracial, post-Christian, self-directed, under-protected, sex-saturated, pandemic generation in history—should be sobering.

It should humble you.

It should intimidate you.

It should weird you out a little.

And it should motivate you to be worth it.

There is nothing like speaking to middle school students. They are this hysterical, interesting gumbo of concrete thinkers melting into the world of the abstract. Someone has wisely observed that middle schoolers are like dogs: They're trying to figure out if you like them. High schoolers, on the other hand, are like cats: They're trying to figure out if they like you. Because of the pandemic, today's middle schooler has been forced to do school on the same device they play Minecraft—which seems a bit like doing CrossFit in a Panda Express. You really haven't lived until you're speaking to a mass of middle schoolers and a girl exasperatedly blurts out **"OH MY GOD!"** to something you say . . . or several middle schoolers frantically raise their hand to either ask you a question or contribute to the discourse—in the middle of your talk.

When you think about it, the fact that a group of pre- and mid-pubescent human beings would sit, squirm, heckle, watch, and listen to a post-pubescent human (you) open their mouth and use orchestrated sounds and movements to paint pictures, tell stories, and transform hearts and minds is insanely fascinating and inspiring in and of itself.

And it also highlights why getting to learn from someone whose years of experience and expertise, making her words weighty and authoritative, is such a gift.

Ashley Bohinc has masterfully created a helpful, practical guide to help you and I become beyond effective in creating a world of faith, hope, and love for middle school students with our words. Of the bazillion things I love about Ashley's detailed labor, the fact that I now have practical, effective handles at the ready to help me eliminate bad habits, nurture best practices, and become a better communicator to middle school students is a game-changer.

Ashley's combined experience of being a public middle school health education teacher, a middle and high school soccer coach, coupled with her years of middle school ministry experience, makes her words more than meaningful. To say she's a bright mind is the grandest of understatements. When she speaks, I listen. I have learned more than I can list from her. Ashley is more than a marginal ministry-world acquaintance. She is a dear friend, my teammate, and a work associate. I have a personal front-row seat to her passion and middle school ministry acumen. We laugh together, and we make each other cry—in a good way. And we respectfully disagree at times, as good teammates should.

Simply stated, Ashley Bohinc is a middle school ministry legend.

One thing you may not know about Ashley is that she's a former college soccer player who has endured multiple injuries because of years playing soccer. You can hear Ashley when she walks in a room. She sounds like a walking Rice Krispy treats commercial. "Snap! Crackle! Pop!"

I would suggest that Ashley's wisdom and expertise on these pages are like her ministry gait after years of experience.

This book is her limp.

And we should always trust someone who walks with a limp.

This year marks my twenty-fourth year of being asked to jump in planes, trains, and automobiles to travel near and far to speak to middle schoolers and high schoolers. Twenty-four years is very deceiving. I don't think I am that good at it. I so badly want to be better at it. I still get intensely nervous before I stand in front of anyone and do it.

To make matters worse, I am painfully introverted (a four with a three wing for you Enneagram cult members), so anytime I do stand in front of others to communicate, it is mentally, emotionally, and physically exhausting—probably because I am having to flap my three wings so hard.

But it is also exhausting because of something Ashley powerfully speaks to in this book:

> "Coach John Wooden was right. Becoming better at whatever it is you're doing requires attention to the smallest details and making changes that might not seem like that big of a deal in the moment. That's true in basketball, and it's true when it comes to communicating to middle schoolers. I like to say it this way: Great middle school communicators aren't 100 percent better than every other communicator. They are one percent better in 100 different ways. All of the things listed in this book are one percent ways to make our delivery better. We have one shot to help this generation of middle schoolers understand a loving God who wants an everyday relationship with each and every one of them."

"We have one shot to help this generation of middle schoolers understand a loving God who wants an everyday relationship with each and every one of them."

I feel the weight of that in my bones.

You should too.

Because our words create worlds.

INTRODUCTION

Heyohhhh!!!

I am so excited you are here.

You are a hero.

Seriously.

Anyone who picks up and opens a book about communicating to middle schoolers deserves a standing ovation.

Because communicating to middle schoolers is not easy.

Maybe you picked up this book because:

⇨ The only thing middle schoolers talk about after you teach your best sermon of all time is that you look really tired, or your teeth look a little yellow today.

⇨ You received feedback from your manager that throwing the microphone against the back wall may not have been the best way to get the attention of your middle schoolers.

⇨ You know the middle school years are important, but you are almost convinced they are more monster than they are human right now.

No matter what the reason is . . .

I'm so glad you did.

And if you have been working with middle schoolers for any length of time, you know this is a wild ride.

Talking to middle schoolers isn't just like talking to big elementary-aged kids,

and it's not like talking to short high schoolers,

and it's certainly not like talking to an adult who forgot to put on deodorant.

It's like talking to a middle schooler.

They are their own unique kind of crazy and awesomeness all wrapped into one! This means if we want to actually reach them with the words we speak, then the way we say them matters a whole lot.

I didn't write this book because I feel like I have all the answers.

In the last 18 years, I have had thousands of conversations with middle schoolers in large groups, in small groups, and one-on-one about topics like puberty, sex, relationships, friendship, authority, decision-making, mental health, family dynamics, goal setting, and choices.

I've gotten it wrong as many times as I've gotten it right.
I have laughed at myself, and at the funny things middle schoolers do, a lot.

As a classroom teacher, I learned some things that I wish every youth pastor knew. After all, when you are with a kid for an hour every single day, in a place they don't want to be, trying to teach them something they don't want to know, you learn some tricks that help keep their attention. At the same time, I've learned some things in ministry I never knew as a teacher—like how to condense life-changing truth to fit into one hour a week, and how to squeeze it in between a dodgeball tournament and pizza.

My experience in both worlds, combined with plenty of trial and error, has gifted me with insights that I've been able to share with ministry leaders around the country to help them become the communicators they want to be.

And that's what I am so excited to share about in this book.

My hope is that in sharing some of the things I have learned along the way—and what others have learned—I can help you lead middle schoolers from exactly where they are to where you want them to be, while avoiding some of our mistakes.

In this book, I am talking specifically about communicating to middle schoolers in a larger group setting:

a classroom,
Sunday school,
in youth group,
on the sideline or locker room to a sports team,
a camp or weekend retreat,
a school or neighborhood-based ministry,
or really, any setting where you would be teaching more than a few middle schoolers.

Although the same principles are true in a smaller group setting (and even true in a one-on-one setting), for the sake of this book, we are talking about teaching middle schoolers from the front of the room or standing on a stage.

You will notice throughout the book there is space to reflect, evaluate, and journal. Why? Because you will need time to contextualize the information for your specific setting, your specific students, and your specific wiring as a communicator. And because . . . well, I'll tell you on page 78.

The reason I care so much about communicating to middle schoolers is because of how a single event impacted me when I was a teenager. While I learned how to follow Jesus in my small group, I became a believer because of what was said from a stage. I fully understood salvation because an adult I didn't know (and who didn't know me) communicated the Gospel of Jesus from the front of a room in a way I could understand and relate to. This person spoke my language, using words I would use, and connected truth to something I had personally experienced or was interested in. At that moment, everything I had been taught about faith in Jesus finally made sense.

That's why I think how you communicate to middle schoolers matters so much.

I don't know of a phase in a kid's life with a larger return on investment than middle school. That's why I've given my life to it and why I care so much about the way we relate to them. Because what hangs in the balance of communicating to a middle schooler in a way that is effective, compelling, and concrete may just change everything for them.

We need people like you,
people who love and believe in middle schoolers,
who believe middle schoolers reflect the image of God just as they are,
and who want to communicate the Gospel in a way that helps middle schoolers develop an everyday faith: a faith that goes with them everywhere, into everything.

What an amazing privilege.

1. KNOW YOUR AUDIENCE

THIS IS MIDDLE SCHOOL

What do you do before you meet someone new for the first time?

Personally, my favorite way to prepare is to . . .

Google them.
Stalk their social media.
See if we have any mutual friends.

I know. It sounds creepy, but I just think it helps to know more about who I'm talking to BEFORE I'm actually talking to them. (Also, don't judge me. You do it too. My Instagram handle is @ashleymariebohinc, by the way.)

I believe this is even more true when it comes to talking to middle schoolers. We need to know who we're actually talking to. If we don't, there's no way we can adequately prepare. Think about it: the way we talk to a 23-year-old about shame and forgiveness is an entirely different conversation than talking to an 11-year-old about it.

So first, let's get on the same page about who we are talking to.

"

A lot goes into a talk, yet the thing every middle school communicator needs to remember is that relationship with your students is more important than everything else. So, in whatever way you can, wherever you can, leverage the relational equity you have with your students at every juncture of your talk. You know your students better than anyone else. Believe that and allow God to work uniquely through you that way!"

—Jamal Jones

JOB	LOCATION	EXPERIENCE
Orange Students Curriculum Guide and Youth Pastor	Richmond, VA, USA	10+ years of experience communicating to middle schoolers

Learn more about how Jamal prepares to communicate on page 245

Depending on geographic location, we all might call this group of humans something different. No matter what you call them—junior highers, pre-teens, youth, high schoolers, or middle schoolers—for the sake of this book, we are talking about students who are 10-14 years old. In the United States, that's typically grades six through eight.

There are two ways we can really know middle schoolers: knowing them culturally and knowing them developmentally.

Knowing middle schoolers *culturally* means knowing . . .

- ⇨ what words are cool (or whatever the latest word for "cool" is at the time you are reading this).
- ⇨ what shows they are watching.
- ⇨ the music they like.
- ⇨ what apps they are using.
- ⇨ the latest challenges and trends on TikTok (or on the app that has already replaced TikTok at the time you are reading this).
- ⇨ the influencers they are following on social media.
- ⇨ the latest fashion trends (even if you'd never wear them).
- ⇨ how their friends view hot topic issues.
- ⇨ what is normal to talk about and what isn't.

I was having a conversation with a girl named Aryanna in the eighth-grade small group I lead, who reminded me of why it's so important to know your middle schoolers culturally. She advised me, "*You have to listen to Nicki Minaj, or you will never be cool. If you go to a party and they are playing Nicki Minaj, and you ask who it is, they'll probably kick you out.*"

Nobody wants to get kicked out of the eighth-grade party!

Getting to know middle school culture is tricky because . . .

Culture changes.
And culture changes fast.

The middle school culture where I live may be totally different from the middle school culture where you are. That's why it's so important to be interacting with middle schoolers as often as possible, because it's hard to really know them unless you know their culture.

Knowing them culturally takes a lot of time and effort, and a desire to learn continuously by reading, researching, and discovering new things. If you don't keep up with what is changing, chances are you'll run the risk of thinking they are the same as you were in middle school and their world is the same as yours was. If we aren't intentional, we lose credibility by talking to them as if they live in a world that no longer exists.

While knowing middle schoolers culturally means you know what's going on around them and how they are collectively influenced by it, knowing middle schoolers *developmentally* looks a little different.

Knowing middle schoolers developmentally means knowing how they are changing **p**hysically, **m**entally, **s**ocially, **e**motionally, and **s**piritually.

Personally, I remember these developmental changes as PMSES . . . (get it?).

1. **Physically**

   Puberty begins, and, well, you know. They start getting taller. Acne is popping up. Voices are starting to change. Deodorant is not only en-couraged, but necessary. Everything is growing. Their body is physi-cally changing from a child to an adult.[1] We have all gone through this, even though you might have tried to block it from your memory.

2. **Mentally**

   As middle schoolers are experiencing the physical changes of puberty, they are simultaneously experiencing a complete rewiring of the brain. In fact, the brain is changing and developing as much, and as fast, right now as it does during the toddler years.[2] As the brain rewires itself, middle schoolers are forgetting more things, more often, because their brain literally cannot remember them. Thanks to a process called *pruning*, middle schoolers lose thousands of neural connections that are no longer needed as new ones grow in. That means they may seem forgetful of certain things because those con-nections in their brain have been eliminated since you told them![3]

   During this time, middle schoolers still primarily think concretely, or literally.

Concrete thinking: a literal form of thinking that focuses on the physical world.

As concrete thinkers, they take what is in front of them at face-value without thinking beyond their own viewpoint or generalizing the information to other meanings or situations. This form of thinking is characterized by the ongoing development of organized and rational thinking. They are able to use logical thought or operations, but they can only apply that logic toward physical objects. Concrete thinking is the opposite of abstract thinking.[4]

Abstract thinking: a more complex, layered form of thinking that goes deeper than the physical information.

Abstract thinking allows for thinking "outside the box." It allows them to make generalizations about something and contemplate concepts that are philosophical and theoretical in nature. They are able to understand and connect words and ideas beyond their literal meaning without help. Abstract thinking is the opposite of concrete thinking.

For most middle schoolers, the brain hasn't yet developed the ability to think abstractly.[5] Like my friends Scott Rubin and Mark Oestreicher brilliantly say, gaining the ability to think abstractly is kind of like a new muscle that is wimpy or weak. You begin to have the ability to think abstractly, but it doesn't happen overnight. Just like a muscle that has to be strengthened in training, you have to practice thinking abstractly, failing sometimes and learning the skill over time to do it well.[6]

What is so incredible about beginning to think abstractly is that this allows middle schoolers to become much more self-aware and able to understand how others may perceive them.[7] At the same time, abstract thinking also allows for an increased ability to not only doubt, but to process doubt in a way they might not have before. These skills are imperative when it comes to developing an everyday faith.

Another way middle schoolers are developing mentally is **they are beginning to realize there's something not beautiful or perfect about themselves.** They start to realize, "Maybe I am not actually a good singer," or "Maybe soccer isn't my sport." With abstract thinking, they become aware of what they can and can't do as they see how others perceive them.

Middle schoolers are thinking more critically than they ever have before. They are deciding if what they have been told is something they believe to be true. They are having to problem-solve things like time management and conflicts with others. At the same time, they are adapting to lots of new changes to their bodies—like growth spurts, body hair, and the sound of their cracking voice. They are adapting to new concepts—like owning their faith as opposed to having a faith that was handed down to them from their grandparent. And they are adapting to new experiences—like their first crush or finally being allowed to go to the out-of-town soccer tournament.

They might not be the best at setting goals, paying attention, or planning.[8] They might seem unmotivated, lack self-control, or appear reckless.[9] The reason they take random risks is because they are mentally unable to comprehend the consequences that may happen in the future as a result of their actions and decisions.[10]

All of these presumed "mental lapses" are controlled by the prefrontal cortex, which is located in the front part of the brain behind the forehead. This part of the brain is not fully developed until around 25 years old, which explains a lot about the behavior of middle schoolers.[11]

3. **Socially**

Middle school is the phase where friendships are changing drastically, and often. Up until this point, friendships have been primarily based on proximity—meaning, their friends were practically assigned based on who lives on their street, who rides their bus, who's in their class, who's on their team, and whose parents are friends with their parents.

Now, they don't have to be friends with the people in their class anymore, and they don't have to be friends with the kid whose parents are friends with their parents. They are choosing friends who aren't necessarily based on proximity but are now based more on affinity. They are choosing their friends based on similar interests, who they like, and where they feel accepted.[12] As those variables change quickly (and regularly), so do their friends and friend groups.

I currently serve as the Director of Middle School Strategy at Orange. Basically, that means I get to be part of a huge team of people who have a heart to resource and influence those who influence the faith of the next generation—church leaders, parents, and volunteers.

A few years ago, Orange launched The Phase Project, a synthesis of personal experience, academic research, and gatherings of leaders and educational experts from across the child development spectrum.[13]

Through The Phase Project, we saw over and over again that middle schoolers are motivated by acceptance, and the one thing they need most during this phase is to be affirmed in their personal journey.[14]

When middle schoolers experience affirmation, their brain releases *dopamine*, which makes them feel something similar to excitement. When middle schoolers receive that social approval from their peers, dopamine is released, and its levels increase higher than they ever have before. Naturally, they want to keep seeking that feeling.

As middle schoolers enter the world of social media, they are entering a whole new world of social approval too. Not only are they seeking acceptance and connection from their peers in person, but also from their peers on their social platforms. For example, if they upload a TikTok and get one hundred likes, that makes them feel good. So naturally, they are going to want to do that more.

4. **Emotionally**

Middle schoolers are certainly not known for their self-regulation of emotions.[15] Think of their emotions like the paint on an artist's palette. Up until puberty begins, they're really only able to experience the three primary colors of emotions: happy, mad, and sad.

When puberty hits, all of a sudden, that artist's palette is filled with colors and emotions they've never experienced before. They have no idea how to express those new emotions or what to do with them. They don't even know how to describe how they feel to somebody. But here's what they do know: What they feel is intense and real, and it's the most important thing. And their emotions are changing FAST.[16]

BEFORE PUBERTY

DURING AND POST-PUBERTY

As middle schoolers begin to experience more than just the three primary emotions, they're figuring out what to do with these new, and often very intense, emotions. They may actually respond more intensely to emotionally-loaded situations because they really don't know what to do with that emotion. This is why it's really important to help them identify what they're feeling, why they're feeling it, and how they can express that emotion in a healthy way.

One way to help middle schoolers develop a vocabulary around their emotions is by introducing them to a Feelings Wheel.[17]

1. Starting in the center, have them pick one core emotion they are feeling from the six options.

2. Then, follow that word section to the middle ring, where that core emotion is broken down into more specific words. Have them pick a more specific word that best describes how they are feeling.

3. From there, follow that specific word out to the outer ring that breaks that specific emotion down into two more specific terms. Encourage them to pick the term that best represents what they are feeling.

This activity will help them build a library of words used to describe how they are feeling. When a middle schooler can better name the emotion they are feeling, we can know how to help them in the best way possible as they navigate it.

FEELINGS WHEEL

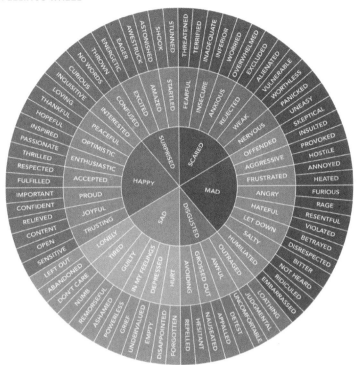

5. Spiritually

The ability to think abstractly is a gift from puberty, which opens up many doors when it comes to their spiritual walk. Since middle schoolers are now able to express doubt, they start asking questions about their faith that they might never have been able to ask before. Like our friends at Fuller Youth Institute say, "doubt is not toxic to faith; silence is."[18] In the process of verbally expressing doubt, they are understanding faith for the very first time for themselves. And this is when they can begin to make their faith their own—when they're able to ask questions and understand an idea on a deeper level, not believing it just because someone else told them to.

"

Teaching is as much about who YOU are as who THEY are as the audience. Know yourself so you can relate to your audience."

—Mikiala Tennie

JOB	LOCATION	EXPERIENCE
Volunteer Youth Leader and Speaker, Church of the Resurrection	Kansas City, KS, USA	17+ years of experience communicating to middle schoolers

Learn more about how Mikiala prepares to communicate on page 232

Middle schoolers are making significant connections to people outside their family for the first time, so this is a great opportunity to introduce them to the idea of community and the way God's family (the Church) is designed to work, not just when they're older but right now. Additionally, as middle schoolers become more self-aware, they start to realize they're not perfect, which can lead them to understand why they need a Savior in the first place. And that is a life-changing opportunity to affirm and celebrate.

If you are anything like me, when you take time to consider all the developmental changes happening in the life of a 10 to 14-year-old, you realize what an incredible window of time this is to positively influence them. It's an honor to have a chance to speak into the life of someone who is changing before our very own eyes.

Here's the thing—you can know middle schoolers culturally, but not know them developmentally. And you can know middle schoolers developmentally, but be totally out of touch with them culturally.

Knowing them in both ways is important because when you do, you can begin to communicate truth in a way that not only makes sense to them right now but in a way that sticks with them as they continue to develop an everyday faith of their own.

Every time you teach a middle schooler, remember that . . .

This isn't an adult sermon with more games.
This isn't a babysitting gig with a devotional.
This isn't a high schooler in training or an overgrown toddler.
This is a unique stage of life with unique opportunities that you have never had before and may never get again.

This is middle school.

Reflect & Contextualize

In your own words, describe the difference between knowing middle schoolers culturally and knowing them developmentally.

_____

_____

_____

On a scale from 1-10, how well do you know middle schoolers culturally?

○——○——○——○——○——○——○——○——○——○
1   2   3   4   5   6   7   8   9   10

Why did you rate yourself with this number?

_____

_____

_____

Pause. Before you move on, spend some time eavesdropping on middle schoolers talking at church, shopping in the Dollar Store, or stalk the comments or posts they make on social media.

Write down words or phrases you hear that you don't know the meaning of and look up the definition. Drop them below:

_____

_____

_____

Ask your middle schoolers the questions below (these will change fast, so ask often):

Shows they are currently watching:

_____

_____

Music they listen to:

_____

_____

Family dynamic:

_____

_____

Apps they are using:

_____

_____

Latest social media challenges and trends:

_____

_____

Athletes they are following:

_____

_____

Influencers they are following:

_____

_____

Latest fashion trends:

_____

_____

How middle schoolers view trending topics (like racial injustice, mental health, environmental concerns):

_____

_____

What do they talk about that surprises you or is different from what you would have talked about at their age?

_____

_____

_____

On a scale from 1-10, how well do you know middle schoolers developmentally?

| 1 | 2 | 3 | 4 | 5 | 6 | 7 | 8 | 9 | 10 |

Why did you rate yourself this number?

_____

_____

_____

What do you think are the top three developmental facts that make communicating to middle schoolers . . .

a challenge:

1. _____

2. _____

3. _____

an incredible opportunity:

1. _____

2. _____

3. _____

Create three descriptive profiles of middle schoolers you will use to reference as you prepare to communicate to middle schoolers:

Profile 1

NAME

AGE

GENDER

GRADE

CITY, STATE, COUNTRY

PHYSICAL DESCRIPTION

MENTAL DESCRIPTION

SOCIAL DESCRIPTION

EMOTIONAL DESCRIPTION

SPIRITUAL DESCRIPTION

FAMILY BACKGROUND

DESCRIPTION OF THEIR INTERESTS CULTURALLY

Profile 2

NAME

AGE

GENDER

GRADE

CITY, STATE, COUNTRY

PHYSICAL DESCRIPTION

MENTAL DESCRIPTION

SOCIAL DESCRIPTION

EMOTIONAL DESCRIPTION

SPIRITUAL DESCRIPTION

FAMILY BACKGROUND

DESCRIPTION OF THEIR INTERESTS CULTURALLY

Profile 3

NAME
....

AGE
....

GENDER
....

GRADE
....

CITY, STATE, COUNTRY
....

PHYSICAL DESCRIPTION
....

MENTAL DESCRIPTION
....

SOCIAL DESCRIPTION
....

EMOTIONAL DESCRIPTION
....

SPIRITUAL DESCRIPTION
....

FAMILY BACKGROUND
....

DESCRIPTION OF THEIR INTERESTS CULTURALLY
....

....

Go to orangestudents.com/feelingswheel and download the
Feelings Wheel for free! Start using it with your middle schoolers.

BREAK IT DOWN

Have you ever heard a youth worker talk about dumbing down the high school content so that middle schoolers can keep up?

The truth is, I get really frustrated when I hear this. I couldn't disagree more.

Because when it comes to communicating to middle schoolers, it's not about *watering down* or *dumbing down* the message; it's about *BREAKING DOWN* the message.

Here's the difference:

Watering down makes something weaker or less effective.	**Dumbing down** lowers the level of difficulty or intelligence.	**Breaking down** separates something into smaller parts.

It's why we cut a hamburger into tiny, bite-sized pieces for a toddler, right? Because they need the nutrition the food brings, but they have to consume it differently than an adult. They can eat the same foods, but we don't want them to choke in the process of receiving the very thing they need to survive. The same thing is true when it comes to helping middle schoolers process their faith: breaking the abstract concepts into smaller pieces helps them digest it.

Middle schoolers are smart. They can handle big things and deep things. And since their brains are changing fast, they process concepts and information in a unique way in this phase. Because of that, we have to break big ideas down into small parts and then show them how they are all connected.

Here's the thing: Most communicators won't do this because it takes more words, and it takes more effort. Speaking in a way that's too complicated for middle schoolers to digest may *seem* deeper or more effective, but in reality, the opposite is true. **Our depth is dependent on how we are able to break information down for middle schoolers.**

This is why I believe with all of my heart that teaching middle schoolers is the most difficult group to teach. And if you master it, I believe you can teach anybody.

CONNECT IDEAS

Breaking it down means **connecting ideas.** Middle schoolers aren't always great at connecting what you talked about first to what you talked about third. You have to help them make that connection. You have to take them along with you as you move from concept to concept, and idea to idea. The way you communicate is more like a connect-the-dots game than a coloring page. If you tell a story, show a picture, or play a YouTube video clip, you will need to connect how that relates to what you are talking about. Don't assume they will make that connection themselves.

That's because middle schoolers think like engineers.[19] Engineers solve problems by connecting concepts that work together. For example, one engineer who's working on a bridge might have to blend information from architecture, politics, environmental science, and construction in order to actually get the job done. That's the same way a middle schooler personalizes abstract concepts. They connect ideas and information to build something that makes sense, so we as leaders have to help them make those connections.

Recently, I was speaking at a student camp teaching John 10:10. I talked about how, oftentimes, we think being a Christian means that we miss out on things. We think we can't dress that way, we can't say those words, and we don't laugh at those kinds of jokes, but the truth is, Jesus didn't come to take away our life—that's what the thief does. Jesus came to bring us life to the full. To illustrate this point, I showed a viral TikTok video of a man speaking at a virtual conference. He started his talk by saying, "Alexa, max volume. Alexa, play 'Who Let the Dogs Out.'" Thousands of Alexas went off simultaneously on max volume in homes across the globe. But here's the thing, that song starts off with a grown man screaming at the top of his lungs, and the music doesn't quiet down at any point. When Alexa is playing that song on max volume, Alexa cannot hear you saying turn it down or turn it off. You have to physically unplug her. Of course, the students were laughing at this stunt that was pulled (and I am sure planning to do this to their own families when they got home), but a great illustration like that can be totally missed if you don't help a middle schooler make the connection by saying, "THAT is the kind of life Jesus wants us to have. Life on MAX VOLUME. Life to the full. A life so full and so loud that nothing can turn it down."

The brains of middle schoolers are meaning-makers. They *want* to be able to connect ideas, but they don't quite know how. It's our job to give them ideas that are not difficult to connect. Connecting ideas takes more words and more effort, but as you do, you'll take your middle schoolers along with you as you move from idea to idea.

IMAGINE THE CONVERSATIONS

Breaking it down means we have to **imagine the conversations** and questions that will come after you communicate. Will your students text about it afterwards? Will they discuss it or remember it at all? Personally, I'm a big fan of small groups meeting immediately after hearing a message, where students have a consistent and safe place to process and wrestle with how the truths they hear apply to their own life, alongside their peers and a trusted, caring adult. **Because our job as the communicator is to connect ideas and set students up for an incredible conversation.** We want them to have conversations about how what they just heard applies to their life, not where someone else is re-teaching the message because we were not clear enough. No matter what I am teaching or writing, I always ask a group of people who work with middle schoolers, "What's the first thing you think they are going to ask when they hear this?"

A couple of years ago, I was preparing to teach a standalone talk on pornography. I wrestled with a middle school appropriate definition of pornography for weeks. I had countless threads of text messages with many people who are much smarter than me. We came up with a definition that we felt was really clear and developmentally appropriate. What I wasn't prepared for was for a middle schooler to claim she knew all about it because "they have been talking about *chromatography* in science class." I don't think I connected the definition we came up with to the content well enough. (My apologies to her science teacher for causing a mix-up of definitions and terms).

This is middle school.

I remember when one of my small group leaders reported that the only thing their small group talked about that day was the difference between gentiles and genitals. So, you can see how first getting into their heads, and then clearly defining words, is super-important.

This is middle school.

I always know when I share a story about an injury in my message that the volunteer leaders are about to hear about every injury their middle schoolers have ever had during small group time. So, when I anticipate something like that happening, I always say something about it upfront. Or I prepare the small group leaders to not only expect that conversation to happen, but equip them with how to navigate around it so it doesn't prevent them from actually talking about the content during their group time.

This is middle school.

I was at a middle school camp years ago, and they were teaching all about how Jesus instructed us to be fishers of men. Afterward, when the service was letting out, I saw a middle school girl pretty distraught. So, I went over to her to ask her what was going on, and she said, "I don't know if I can do what Jesus asked. I don't know how to fish, and I don't know any men."

This is middle school.

Each rotation in Health class, I taught about skin cancer and the "ABCDE" warning signs of cancerous moles. As I wrapped up the lesson, they were broken up into pairs to work on a project, and, one by one, a sixth grader would walk up to me, show me a mole on their body, and ask if they should be concerned.

This is middle school.

One time I was teaching a lesson on the parable of the talents. A middle schooler went home, and their parents asked what they learned about. Their response was, "I don't know, but you shouldn't bury anything in the backyard."

This is middle school.

Middle schoolers are amazing, aren't they? That's why, in our preparation (which is coming in a later chapter), we need to imagine the conversations and questions that will happen afterward, so we remove any obstacle for them to have a helpful discussion about how that truth intersects with their everyday life.

CATEGORIZE

Breaking it down means **categorizing.** Have you ever felt like no matter how many different questions you asked a middle schooler, they were only giving you one-word answers? Or their answers were really vague? Like the conversation would just die every time you tried to get something out of them?

One of the most helpful things I have learned about communicating to middle schoolers is this: **If you ask them too broad of a question, they don't know what you are actually asking.**

Open-ended questions are important, but if you give them a category to place your question, they are more likely to follow your train of thought or have an answer for you. It's like providing a structure to ask an open-ended question.

It's kind of like sorting our trash.

We have a bin for trash, a bin for paper, a bin for plastic, and a bin for compost. Think of it like this: Each bin represents a part of middle schoolers' life: Family, school, friends, and hobbies.

If you ask a middle schooler, "How can you show people you care about them?" you may not get great answers. I mean, there are many different ways to show different people you care about them! And how a middle schooler would say they show their family they care about them may be a totally different answer than how they might show their neighbor they care about them.

Like we said earlier, middle schoolers are still developing the ability to think in layers. They may not even be able to identify the layers to the question. So, if you categorize the question, chances are you will get a better response because they know what you are actually asking and how to think about it.

So instead of asking, "How can you show people you care about them?" you might ask these four questions one at a time instead:

How can you show **your friends** you care about them?
How can you show **your family** you care about them?
How can you show **your teammates** you care about them?
How can you show **your neighbors** you care about them?

This is true in a large group setting, a small group setting, or a one-on-one conversation with a middle schooler.

Categorizing takes more words, and it takes more effort for the one asking questions. But when we put big questions and ideas into categories for middle schoolers, we're breaking it down in a way that will get better answers and set up better conversations.

PRESENT ONE IDEA

Breaking it down means **presenting one idea at a time.** One of the most helpful things I was taught in my education classes was the importance of NOT stacking ideas or questions. Instead, ask one question at a time, and present one idea at a time.

Stacking directions might look something like this:

"I want you to stand up, grab a marker, and write 'I am love' on the bottom of your shoe. When you are done, come to the back of the room for a picture."

Wait. What?

A way to break down these directions so that they are not stacked might look like this:

"Everyone, stand up!" (Allow time for everyone to do that.)

"Come grab a marker." (Wait to give the next instruction until everyone has a marker in their hand.)

"Now, everyone, take one minute and write 'I am loved' on the bottom of your shoe." (Give everyone one minute to do that.)

"As you finish, come to the back of the room for a picture."

By breaking down these instructions, you are giving them time to process what you want them to do. The same thing goes for asking questions.

Stacking questions might look something like this:

"Have you ever been in a fight with your sibling? What happened? How did that make you feel? Did you react when that happened? What would have been a healthier way to react?"

That's five questions, not one. A middle schooler has no idea which question to answer first. And then, they have to figure out how all those questions relate to each other. It would be better for a middle schooler's brain to ask one question at a time, giving them time to answer after each, and then help them connect the questions together on the back end, not the front end.

This is also why it's important to pick one bottom line and one main point for your lesson. Stacking ideas on a middle schooler will result in them not remembering or understanding any of the ideas.

Every time you teach a middle schooler, remember to **break it down.**

Reflect & Contextualize

Have you ever used the words "dumb it down" or "water it down" to describe communicating to middle schoolers?

_____ Guilty   _____ Not Guilty

Have you ever stacked directions when communicating to middle schoolers?

_____ Guilty   _____ Not Guilty

Practice unstacking the instructions below and write in where the communicator should pause (and let the students actually do that thing first) before moving on:

"Everyone find a partner, sit down somewhere next to each other, talk about the first question on the screen, come up with one word to describe your conversation, and write it on this poster up front."

_____

_____

_____

"I am going to put four pictures up on the screen. When I do, you pick which of these pictures you identify with most, and move to the corners of the room that match the corners the pictures are in."

_____

_____

_____

"I want you to picture a scenario in your mind where you wish there were no rules, then you are going to talk about it with the person to the right of you."

_____

_____

_____

Practice unstacking the questions below:

"What's a change you went through recently and how did it make you feel?

_____

_____

"What do you think it means to be resilient and how resilient do you think you are? Who is someone else you know who is resilient and how did they become resilient?"

_____

_____

"How does it make you feel to know that you are made in the image of God and that God thinks you are a masterpiece?"

_____

_____

Think about the last game you played or the last activity you led your middle schoolers through. Practice unstacking the directions to the game/activity below:

_____

_____

_____

_____

_____

_____

_____

_____

_____

Write down a story that illustrates a time when a middle schooler didn't connect the story you told to the point of the message.

_____

_____

_____

_____

_____

_____

_____

_____

Brainstorm some specific questions you could ask a middle schooler in some of the main categories of their life:

FRIENDS

_____

_____

_____

FAMILY

_____

_____

_____

SCHOOL

_____

_____

_____

HOBBIES

_____

_____

_____

OTHER

_____

_____

_____

WORDS MATTER

My dear friend Charlie Conder, one of the best middle school communicators I know, tells a story about a student who was upset because his mom thought he was coming to church to hear about Jesus, and they were singing songs about "Yahweh" instead. He had tears welling in his eyes because he loved coming to youth group so much, but he knew his mom wouldn't be happy.

This is why words matter so much in middle school.

Middle schoolers need us to define words and connect what those words mean to the point we're trying to make. It's not a natural thing to do. It's a skill that even those of us who have been teaching middle schoolers for 15+ years are still learning how to do better.

WORDS MATTER, SO CHOOSE CONCRETE WORDS.

Concrete words are necessary because middle schoolers are still only able to think very concretely and literally. Their ability to think abstractly is still being developed, meaning they are not able to understand and connect words and ideas beyond their literal meaning.

So, this means don't use a ten-dollar word when a ten-cent word would suffice (see what I did there?). And don't use two words when one word works.

ABSTRACT

↑ Produce
　Fruit
　Apple
　Red apple
　Honeycrisp apple
↓ The Honeycrisp apple your mother packed you for lunch

CONCRETE

ABSTRACT

↑ Natural World

Creation

Nature

Plants and animals

My family's pets and plants

↓ My puppy named Rain and my plant named Dotty

CONCRETE

ABSTRACT

↑ Sin

Mistakes

Things you do that you don't want people to know about

The lie you told to your parent on Saturday

Telling your stepdad you were at Gus's house, when you were really

↓ at Amaya's house

CONCRETE

ABSTRACT

↑ Messiah

The Savior of the world

God's Son

↓ Jesus

CONCRETE

ABSTRACT

↑ Church (capital C)

Believers

Christians

People who believe Jesus is the Son of God

LifePoint Church

↓ The 7th-grade boys small group leader, Abel

CONCRETE

Reflect & Contextualize

Listed below are some words we hear often in church. Practice the skill of breaking them down into more concrete language and building up to more abstract language.

Need help? Imagine the profiles of the kids you created previously. How would you describe this word or phrase to them in words they would understand?

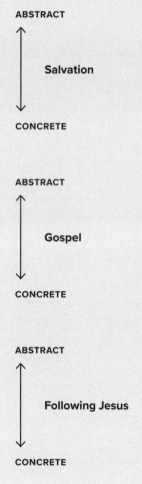

ABSTRACT

Salvation

CONCRETE

ABSTRACT

Gospel

CONCRETE

ABSTRACT

Following Jesus

CONCRETE

ABSTRACT

↑

Trusting Jesus

↓

CONCRETE

ABSTRACT

↑

Family

↓

CONCRETE

ABSTRACT

↑

Potential

↓

CONCRETE

ABSTRACT

↑

Identity

↓

CONCRETE

WORDS MATTER, SO DEFINE WORDS AND PHRASES.

Yes, it will take more words and more time. It might even require you to wrestle with how to break a word down in a concrete way.

While this is not a complete list, here is how I might break down some common words middle schoolers may not understand without an explanation:

Word	How I Might Say It to a Middle Schooler
Mercy	When someone doesn't get the punishment they deserve
Sacrifice	When someone does something hard or painful so that you don't have to
Grace	When God gives us what we don't deserve
Worthy	Enough
Bondage	Weighed down
Fellowship	Spending time together
Praise	Celebrate
Humble/Humbly	To put someone else before yourself
Application	This is what you are supposed to do with the information
Embrace	Hold
Honor	Respect
Meditate	Think about
Mediate	Help two or more people resolve a problem or conflict
Discern	To figure out or decide
Yearn	To want
Sustain	To keep strong, to help you keep going

Yahweh	Jesus
Reconcile	To make it right
Repentance	To admit you were wrong and start doing the right thing
Holiness	Being more like God
Intercede	Step in
Intercessory Prayer	A prayer for someone else's needs
Gospel	Good news

Although it's true there will be some middle schoolers who understand some of (or all of) these words or phrases, the majority of middle schoolers—the average middle schooler—won't.

Duffy Robbins said it best: **"I've come to realize that if teenagers can't understand my content, then they won't be motivated to study God's Word on their own."**[20]

When you are speaking to a room full of middle schoolers, you want to say what you mean in a way that everyone in the room can understand, no matter their listening comprehension level.

Keep in mind that reading comprehension is different from listening comprehension. Just because a middle schooler might read at a seventh-grade level doesn't necessarily mean they listen at a seventh-grade level too. Actually, they might only listen at a third-grade level. Just because they can recognize a word on a multiple-choice vocabulary test doesn't mean they use it regularly in conversation. If you ask them, "Do you know this word?" they'll say, "Yes" because they technically know the definition, but if you use it in conversation, their brain has to go into the archives, find the academic definition, and apply it to the situation. That takes time, and by then, you've already moved on in your talk, and they're lost. So, when you're teaching, you might feel like you are talking in a way that's too "basic." But if you don't, they won't be able to follow you.[21]

WORDS MATTER, SO BE CAREFUL WITH USING WORDS THAT ARE BORDERLINE.

Borderline: on the edge of either being appropriate or going too far.

I was in my early twenties at the first student summer camp I was ever a part of as a leader. I was still a full-time teacher in the public schools, but I was volunteering in the middle school ministry. After the first evening session, Jason, the youth pastor of the ministry, wanted to clarify some theological things that the speaker had said. He asked me to take all of the middle schoolers into one building, and he was going to take the high schoolers into another. Of course, I said yes, but on the walk over to the building, I quickly realized I had no idea how to lead this conversation.

I understood what I needed to clarify about what the speaker said, but I didn't know how to have this conversation with middle schoolers. I didn't know how to break down such an abstract spiritual, theological concept. So, I prayed. I asked for courage and clarity, and when I walked into the building, I started off by asking the group of middle schoolers what they thought about that night's message. A sixth-grade boy named Asael in the front row raised his hand. He asked, "Well, I don't understand why he kept cussing."

I paused for a moment, wondering if we had been in the same room. Cussing? I was so confused; I did not hear the speaker cuss at all! I only heard the speaker explain his theological view of salvation. I paused, and the room was completely silent. Simon, the boy sitting next to him, helped clarify: "The speaker kept saying 'sucks.'"

OHHHHHHH. Got it. I just adore sixth graders. The rest of the conversation was about the word "sucks," why it was okay for some people to use it, but not for others, and why someone would use a word like that in church. This was absolutely not the conversation I was expecting to have. Needless to say, the entire message was so abstract with zero concrete handlebars that it went over their heads completely. And even if there were a few theological concepts that connected, have you ever noticed how middle schoolers tend to fixate on the silly or the questionable? This is why a fart or burp can derail the whole thing. For this crew, the word "suck" was what stuck.

WORDS MATTER, SO KEEP IN MIND THAT BORDERLINE WORDS COULD BE CULTURAL.

Another summer, I was a speaker at a student camp, and the band I was serving with was from another country. They told me that when they first started touring in the USA, they prayed the words, "God, I am such a little a**hole. Forgive me, Father" from the stage. Apparently, that's not considered inappropriate in their specific culture. There's no question anyone who heard that prayer in the United States will remember it for all of eternity.

The point is, keep in mind that what you consider borderline or "okay to say" may be really different for a middle schooler who has been told otherwise.

This is especially true at Christmas. In my humble opinion, Santa Claus is considered a borderline word for middle school—meaning, some middle schoolers still believe in Santa. I know, I know . . . How? I don't understand how, but they do. So, I have made a covenant with myself that I will never speak the truth about Mr. Claus from a stage in front of middle schoolers. It's not my place. It's their parent's place. So, I will continue to talk about all of the other Christmas things instead.

WORDS MATTER, SO BE INTENTIONAL WHEN TALKING ABOUT PARENTS.

When trying to relate to and build trust with middle schoolers, it can be easy to naturally talk about their parents in a way that the middle schooler agrees and identifies with.

"When I was in middle school, my parents were so annoying too."

"Maybe your mom is so strict and doesn't ever let you do anything with your friends."

"Parents are the worst!"

Making a parent the butt of the joke may be one of the quickest and cheapest ways to relate to a middle schooler. But it's also one of the most damaging. When a middle schooler hears this kind of put down, it makes the parent the enemy. As the biggest and most important influence in a kid's life, this is the worst thing we could do for that relationship. We have to think bigger picture than wanting to "seem cool" in that moment.

As middle schoolers crave more independence and more freedom, the space between them and their parent is increasing. They are beginning to question (at least internally) their parents' actions, beliefs, and rules in a way they haven't before. This phase is a time when a kid and a parent begin to naturally experience tension in their relationship.

As communicators, we don't win if we make the gap between a kid and their parent even wider. Making the parent the enemy in the eyes of a kid will only cause the parent to lose trust in us. **We only win as communicators when we help bridge the gap between a middle schooler and the parent—the person who has the greatest influence in their life.**

The vocabulary we use when we talk about family matters a lot, especially for the kid experiencing a non-traditional family dynamic. It can be easy to default to using examples that acknowledge the kid with a mom and dad who are married. But according to the Census Bureau's Current Population Survey conducted in 2020, only about 70 percent of children under the age of 18 live with two parents in the home.[22] A growing number of the kids in our ministries will have lived with one parent and a cohabitating, unmarried, non-parent by the time they graduate high school.

Specifically, when we are giving examples and talking about parents, it's important to keep in mind the kid . . .

with both parents who are married.
with divorced parents.
with the single mom.
with the single dad.
with step-parents.
with two moms, and two step-moms.
with two dads.

whose legal guardians are their grandparents or other family members.

whose legal guardian is another caring adult in their life.

who lives with a foster parent.

with adoptive parents.

who has a strained relationship with one or both parents.

who has no relationship with one or both parents.

whose parents have passed away.

There are many more situations that are not listed here—every kid's situation is different and unique to their family. By giving examples that acknowledge a variety of family and parental dynamics in a way that honors the parent, the kid, and the family, you are letting a kid know you see them in their unique situation, and you are letting the parent or caregiver know you see them too.

WORDS MATTER, SO BE CAUTIOUS WHEN USING METAPHORS.

Metaphor: a word or phrase for one thing that is used to refer to another thing in order to show or suggest they are similar. An object, activity, or idea that is used as a symbol of something else.[23]

Metaphors are very important, so I am not saying you shouldn't use metaphors at all. But when you do use them, keep in mind that middle schoolers are just beginning to realize how to take something that's subjective and make it objective. They are learning how to take something that's "kind of" what we're talking about, and apply it to their lives. When you choose to use metaphors, make sure you're very, very clear about what the metaphor actually means. First, explain what a metaphor is. Then, make sure you connect the dots for them. It might seem like an obvious connection, but for some, it's not.

Here's what I mean. I was teaching about Hebrews 5:12-14, which includes a metaphor using milk and solid food to talk about growing in faith.

You have been believers so long now that you ought to be teaching others. Instead, you need someone to teach you again the basic things about God's word. You are like babies who need milk and cannot eat solid food. For someone who lives on milk is still an infant and doesn't know how to do what is right. Solid food is for those who are mature, who through training have the skill to recognize the difference between right and wrong (Hebrews 5:12-14 NLT) [23]

For an adult, it's easy to see that this is a metaphor, but without some help, a seventh-grader may assume this passage is about eating literal food! It can be helpful to break it down this way:

> "The writer is using milk and solid food to represent something else here. In your English/Language Arts class, you'd call this a metaphor. That's when a writer says that one thing is actually something else in order to explain an idea. So, in this metaphor, milk and solid food don't actually mean milk and solid food. Here, milk and solid food mean the kinds of daily habits we have to grow in our faith.
>
> Milk represents the easy things we can do to learn about God. They're the simple things we can do to help us grow in our faith. And solid food represents the more complicated or even advanced things we can do to learn about God. They're the habits we can develop that will really challenge and strengthen our faith."

Using metaphors takes more words and more effort. But by explaining what a metaphor is, and breaking down the metaphor, we're helping middle schoolers connect and understand ideas in a way that they maybe haven't before.

WORDS MATTER, SO AVOID IDIOMS.

> **Idiom:** an expression that cannot be understood from the meanings of its separate words but that has a separate meaning of its own.[25]

Middle schoolers have difficulty understanding something that has a figurative meaning, not a literal meaning. I honestly never realized how many idioms we have in the English language until I found myself consistently breaking down the meaning of what I was actually saying to someone who spoke English as their second language. That was a lightbulb moment for me. It was then that I realized, "OH, that's why middle schoolers have trouble with these statements. They don't actually mean what I am saying." And depending on your age, you might be using idioms that only connect with a certain age demographic. Saying "here is the 411," or "somebody drank the Kool-Aid" might resonate with middle-aged adults, but not middle schoolers. Be careful to avoid idiomatic phrases that are dated.

While this is not an exhaustive list, here are some ideas of how I might rephrase an idiom for a middle schooler:[24]

Idiom	How I Might Say It to a Middle Schooler
Foot in the mouth	Said something I wish I hadn't said
Break a leg	Do a good job
Strength in numbers	The more of us doing it, the more powerful we are
Takes one to know one	You're just as bad as I am
A blessing in disguise	A good thing that you might not realize is a good thing until later
Better late than never	It's good to do it later than you're supposed to instead of not doing it at all
Call it a day	Let's be done
Cut somebody some slack	Don't be so tough on somebody
Cutting corners	Doing something poorly to save time or money
Getting out of hand	Getting out of control

Get it out of your	Do it now so then you don't do it again
Give someone the benefit of the doubt	Trust what someone says
Get your act together	Do it better or leave
Back to the drawing board	Go back to the beginning to think of a new way to do something
Hang in there	Don't give up
Long story short	To tell something quickly
Miss the boat	It's too late
Pull yourself together	Calm down
The last straw	To be out of patience
Best of both worlds	The perfect situation or combination of things
To make matters worse	To make things worse
Crossing that bridge	Dealing with something when it's time to
Wrap your head around something	Trying to understand something
You can say that again	I completely agree
Perfect storm	The worst possible situation
Game-changer	Something or someone that changes everything
When it rains, it pours	Everything is going wrong at the same time
Actions speak louder than words	Believe what people do and not what they say
Add insult to injury	Make a bad situation worse

Comparing apples to oranges	Comparing things that aren't the same, so you can't really compare them
Do unto others as you would have them do unto you	Treat others the way you want to be treated
Giving someone the cold shoulder	Ignore someone
Piece of cake	Easy
Rain on somebody's parade	Stopping someone from having a good time
Take it with a grain of salt	Don't take it too seriously
Looking through the lens of	See something in a different way
Domino effect	When something happens and it causes something else to happen because of it, and so on . . .
Get a second wind	Get a burst of energy after being tired
On the fence about	Not sure about
Like riding a bike	Something you never forget how to do
On cloud nine	Very happy
Run like the wind	Run fast
Through thick and thin	In good times and in bad times
A leap of faith	Taking a risk and trusting that things will work out
Faith can move mountains	Having faith can make things possible that seem impossible

Think of it as a	Something you can do to not follow a rule
I mean that literally	I mean it exactly as I said it
It floored me	It completely surprised me
Still on the table	Still a possibility
Pushing the envelope	Doing something against the rules to see how much you can actually do before getting into trouble
You killed it	You did a really good job

WORDS MATTER, SO AVOID USING CHRISTIAN WORDS AND PHRASES WITHOUT AN EXPLANATION.

What's fascinating to me is that the New Testament was originally written in *Koine Greek*, the everyday language of ordinary people.[25] This tells me that the greatest news in the whole world can be communicated without a specialized religious vocabulary.

Unfortunately, in modern church world, it can be so easy to use insider language rather than all-inclusive language. Words like "grace," and "mercy," and "fellowship," and "worship," are words that come up all the time in Christian culture, and we don't often stop to consider that middle schoolers—or people raised outside the church—may not really know what they mean. They know the word, but they may not be able to explain what it means or understand how it relates to their everyday life.

This is especially true when it comes to worship songs. Think about it: Lyrics like "covered in the blood of the Lamb," and "no longer a slave to fear," or "start a fire in me, let the flames run free" when you live in an area prone to destructive wildfires can do more harm than good.

Taken literally without any explanation for what they mean, these words can sound a little terrifying, not inspiring.

It can be easy to assume that middle schoolers know what we're talking about when we are teaching about the major historical events that were recorded in the Bible. Middle schoolers may not know what "the story of Easter" or "Noah's Ark" mean, because they were not raised in church. By breaking down what actually happened, even though it takes more words and more time, your students will have a better grasp of that real event, especially if they weren't familiar with it before.

While this is not a complete list, here is how I might rephrase some common Christian phrases:

Phrase	How I Might Say It to a Middle Schooler
Let Jesus lead you toward . . .	Be open to what Jesus wants to do in your life
Battle with . . .	Fight against
On your behalf . . .	For you
In awe of	Amazed by
Pray through something	Pray about something
Seek wisdom	Wanting to know what the wise thing to do is
Covered in the blood	Jesus already did that for you
This verse is housed in . . .	This verse was written by _____ to _____ and we can find it in the book of the Bible called _____.
No longer a slave	It doesn't have control over you anymore
In light of	Because of . . .
Seasoned with	Sprinkled with a little . . .
Out of character for us . . .	Not something we would usually do or say

What hangs in the	What might happen if we don't do this
Bear the weight . . .	Carry worries
Love our global neighbors	Love everyone, no matter where they live in the world
Fall short	We don't do what someone wanted us to do
Sacrifice	Exchange one thing for something else
Spirit-led	Ask God to help you
God knows your heart	God knows what you mean
All hearts and minds clear	Is there anything you'd like to say before we leave today?

WORDS MATTER, AND THAT MEANS BIBLE TRANSLATION MATTERS TOO.

One thing that tends to confuse new believers (and if we're being honest, long-time believers) is deciding which translation of the Bible to use. Some denominations swear by one specific translation, some have a personal preference for when they're studying at home, and some translations are just more well-known than others. I'm not going to tell you which translation to use, but I will tell you some are more helpful than others when you're doing an in-depth study, casually reading for yourself, or preparing to communicate to middle schoolers.

When preparing to communicate to middle schoolers, choose the translation that makes the most sense to a middle schooler, not the one you prefer as an adult.

The first step in doing that? We have to know just what a translation *is*. The Bible has not only been translated into several different languages (hundreds in fact!), it's been translated into specific written language that would best help the reader to understand its meaning. For example, a verse from the *King James Version*[26] may contain words or phrases that aren't used very often anymore (words like "thou" and "thee"), which may make it hard for a middle schooler to understand what exactly is being said. Using a more modern translation that contains words and phrases more commonly used today, like the *New Living Translation,*[27] may help your students to more easily understand what the Scripture means. After all, **the goal is for middle schoolers to understand the Good News, not be more confused by it.**

We also need to be using a translation of Scripture (if at all possible) that middle schoolers can understand and gain as much context as possible.

I was teaching middle schoolers Acts 1:8 recently. As I was preparing, I was looking at the different translations thinking about this. I was looking specifically at the NIV and NLT translations:

> Acts 1:8 (NIV)
> *"But you will receive power when the Holy Spirit comes on you; and you will be my witnesses in Jerusalem, and in all Judea and Samaria, and to the ends of the earth."*[28]

> Acts 1:8 (NLT)
> *"But you will receive power when the Holy Spirit comes upon you. And you will be my witnesses, telling people about me everywhere— in Jerusalem, throughout Judea, in Samaria, and to the ends of the earth."*[29]

Observation #1:
As youth workers, one of our jobs is to think dirty. It's weird, right? We need to anticipate an inappropriate innuendo, a slang term, or a dirty joke, so it doesn't derail the lesson. If you noticed, the NLT uses the phrase "comes upon you" rather than the NIV translation "comes on you." Now, this will either totally go over a middle schooler's head, or it will distract from the point you are trying to make. In my opinion, it isn't worth the risk.

Observation #2:
Both translations use the word "witnesses," however, the NLT provides a definition of a witness in the translation: "telling people about me everywhere." This is a good example of how you break down Scripture so a middle schooler better understands what Jesus is telling them to do.

Observation #3:

Selecting a translation with the most concrete terms and definitions is imperative. However, I have to go one step further and break down the following words included in the verse: power, Holy Spirit, comes upon you, Jerusalem, Judea, Samaria, and to the ends of the earth. Giving context to each of those words and phrases will help a middle schooler connect the dots to what Jesus was actually saying.

One translation isn't better than another. They each breathe new life into Scripture. I appreciate them all, and I don't just stick with one translation. When preparing a lesson, I always look through a handful of different translations to figure out which one breaks down the truth in a way that's the most middle-school-friendly.

As communicators, we have the honor of sharing the greatest message in the entire world with middle schoolers through **words.** The ones we choose to use can either inspire a middle schooler and help them process their faith in a new way, or confuse them as they struggle to understand what we mean. So, in the process, let's intentionally choose words that are portable and broken down so a middle schooler can remember and carry them with them when they leave our doors.

It takes more time, and it takes more effort.

But our words have the potential to help a middle schooler understand God, understand themselves, and understand others in a way that could change everything for them.

So remember, every time you teach a middle schooler, your **words matter.**

Reflect & Contextualize

Brainstorm as many additional idioms, words, or Christian phrases that are not mentioned above, and describe how you might break them down for a middle schooler:

_____

_____

_____

_____

_____

_____

_____

Go back through the last three talks you gave. Either go back to your notes or listen to each one, if they are recorded. Did you use any words or phrases your middle schoolers may not have fully understood? List them below, along with a better choice of words for next time.

_____

_____

_____

_____

_____

_____

_____

Look up the Scripture verses you will be teaching soon, or have taught recently, in five different translations.

Which translation do you think would work best to teach middle schoolers? Why?

_____

_____

_____

_____

_____

_____

What words or phrases in that Scripture will you need to explain or break down no matter what? How will you do that?

_____

_____

_____

_____

_____

_____

_____

_____

_____

_____

_____

2. DEVELOP YOUR PIECES

Before we even get to developing the pieces, the parts of the content that make up your message, let's talk briefly about the foundation of the content.

> **Hermeneutics:** a method or principle of interpretation.[32]

So many communicators stop at **hermeneutics**—asking the question, "Is my sermon true? Is this an appropriate interpretation of the text?" Interpreting the truth is VERY important, but if no one remembers it (or understands it), it isn't effective because it doesn't create life change.

While hermeneutics matter, this is a book about **homiletics.**

> **Homiletics:** the art of preaching.[33]

More specifically, this book is about **developmental homiletics** toward one audience—middle schoolers.

"

Find a way of communicating that is right for you. There isn't one right way to do it. If you like to draw, use it in how you communicate. If you like music and create songs, use it in how you communicate. If you like graphs and data, use it in how you communicate. We all have unique ways in which we communicate. It doesn't have to be just words on a screen. Use your unique giftings to make your talk a reflection of who you are and who God has created you to be."

—Jean Sohn

JOB	LOCATION	EXPERIENCE
Middle School Director at Gwinnett Church	Atlanta, GA, USA	8+ years of experience communicating to middle schoolers

Learn more about how Jean prepares to communicate on page 250

> **Developmental homiletics:** the art of preaching in a way that is effectively broken down and delivered in a way that sticks for a specific phase.

This means every piece of content we plan to deliver needs to be true, but it also needs to be effectively delivered—and broken down—in a way that is helpful and memorable to a middle schooler.

So, with that in mind, let's start developing the pieces of your message for middle schoolers!

THINK BIG PICTURE

It's easy to grow tired of teaching the same thing over and over again. I know I am guilty of having that thought on more than one occasion. However, the more I learn about how the brain processes information, the more convinced I become of the need for spiritual truths to be cyclical in nature.

Will you nerd out on neuroscience with me for just a moment?

Learning takes place when two neurons in the brain communicate with each other. The brain is magnificently wired in a way that, when we say truths like, "God loves you," many neurons connect for the middle schooler's brain to understand this message. When those neurons connect repeatedly, the brain forms a neural network around that piece of information. The more a middle schooler hears, "God loves you," their brain eventually becomes so accustomed to firing neurons together around that truth that it becomes difficult to change this information in their brain later in life. It is often said that "neurons that fire together wire together."[32] We, as leaders, have the amazing privilege of hardwiring spiritual truths into the brain of middle schoolers. Isn't that incredible?!

As the Director of Middle School Strategy at Orange, I get to work with, collaborate with, and dream with some of my favorite people who have a heart to reach middle schoolers across the globe by creating incredible resources for church leaders, parents, and volunteers.

One of the ways we think big picture at Orange Students is through our three-year Scope and Cycle. This is basically our "road map" for our middle school and high school curriculums.

> **Scope:** the comprehensive plan that prioritizes *what* you teach and *when*.

> **Cycle:** the plan to recycle or revisit what you teach to make sure what you're teaching sticks effectively.

When developing every three-year Scope and Cycle, we consider things like the rhythm of the family and teenagers, the school calendar, holidays, etc. We also strategically place sensitive topics like sexual integrity to happen at specific times in the year.[33]

I really believe in this strategic approach to teaching, but I also know that you know your students best. You know what they need to talk about and when they need to talk about it. The Scope and Cycle we use is just a suggestion based on these filters we find consistent in teenagers around the globe. But you, as a ministry leader, will need to develop a plan that works for your specific context. Because just like our lives are made healthier by balance, so are our ministries. Following a Scope and Cycle offers your ministry the balance and focus it needs to ensure you're teaching your students what they need to know when they need it in a way they can apply as they grow.

Every time you prepare to teach a middle schooler, remember to **think big picture**, always keeping in focus what you want them to know when they leave your ministry.

Reflect & Contextualize

Pause.

Put this book down.

Look at your calendar and schedule two hours to think about and re-evaluate the big picture of your ministry. When it's on your calendar, come back.

What's your big picture plan?

_____

_____

_____

_____

_____

_____

_____

_____

_____

_____

_____

_____

If you aren't sure, that's okay!
Go to Orangestudents.com/plan and borrow ours!

CONTEXTUALIZE

Have you ever found yourself having to teach the same message to two totally different groups of students?

- ⇨ The first group is quiet and disengaged, but the second group won't stop talking.
- ⇨ The Wednesday night gathering is all church kids, and the Sunday service is mostly guests and middle schoolers who are new to church.
- ⇨ One kid shows up to the Saturday evening service, and 30 kids show up to the Sunday morning service.
- ⇨ The Fellowship of Christian Athletes club at one campus has a consistent group of kids showing up, and the club at another seems to have different kids showing up every time.

It's complicated, right?

My Saturday service DID start with one student and four leaders showing up, and my Sunday service started with 30 students. The dynamics in these two environments were wildly different. I felt badly for the one student who showed up on Saturday, because they were outnumbered and overwhelmed with adults. I quickly learned that snapping on a microphone, and standing up to teach like I do on Sunday mornings, resulted in that one kid feeling like they were in trouble and not wanting to show up to church again.

Obviously, it depends on the personality of that one middle schooler, right? We both know middle schoolers who would thrive in being the center of attention. (Why are their names always Christian or Madison?) We also both know some middle schoolers who would fake an illness just so their parents would not make them have to go to Saturday church again.

No matter the personality of the kid, the truth is the way I needed to deliver the information needed to be drastically different. How was I supposed to take one curriculum and make it work for both one kid on Saturday or 30 kids on Sunday?

Maybe you use a curriculum like I did. Or maybe you have time to write your own. Awesome! No matter where your curriculum comes from, contextualizing it will make it more helpful to you *and* your students.

> **Context:** the situation in which something happens.[36]

> **Contextualize:** to place something, such as a word or activity, in a context.[37]

The truth is, no one person can write a curriculum for every context. Even if you heard a sermon and it was awesome, you may repeat it to your students and it doesn't work. You may have read an illustration that was bomb, but if your students don't connect with it, it doesn't help them. **Context is everything.** So, contextualize, contextualize, contextualize.

The very best communicators I have observed approach their curriculum asking these kinds of questions:

⇨ Will this work with my students?

⇨ Do my students need more background before we get to this point?

⇨ Will this work in my physical space with the number of students I have?

⇨ Do my students know this movie, TV show, book reference, etc.?

⇨ How can I make this resonate with both the guys and gals in the room?

⇨ Is my group made up of sixth grade through eighth grade? Fifth grade through ninth grade? Just seventh and eighth grade? How might the content need to change to hit all of those grade levels? Or how can I address each grade individually?

⇨ Is there anything I need to prep my leaders on to have the best possible conversation following my lesson?

⇨ What does my denomination believe about this particular truth?

⇨ Does my denomination prefer I use a different translation of Scripture?

⇨ Do I want to add any supporting Scripture references that my students or denomination would connect with best?

⇨ Does this application hit every kid in my youth group?

⇨ Have I considered the kid in my group who _____?

⇨ Does this use any words that might be a trigger for my students?

⇨ What will parents in this region of the world think about me saying this?

⇨ Did something just happen in my community that is a great example of this?

⇨ Does this consider a kid who was raised in church?

⇨ Does this consider a kid who is brand-new to faith?

⇨ Have I considered my students with special needs?

⇨ How can I make this feel less like I am talking AT them, but more like I am talking WITH them?

Every time you teach middle schoolers, remember to **contextualize**. Every single curriculum needs to be contextualized. There is no "plug and play" when it comes to middle school ministry. **You know your students better than anyone.** You know your denomination better than anyone. You know which translation of Scripture your church prefers to use. **Curriculum is always a starting line—you take it to the finish line.**

Reflect & Contextualize

Do you find yourself having multiple environments that are very different from each other? How so?

_____

_____

_____

Whether you're writing your own or using a curriculum, how well do you feel like you are contextualizing your content for your unique environment?

_____

_____

_____

Who can you invite into the process to help you better contextualize?

1. _____

2. _____

3. _____

PAUSE and pull up your calendar.

Block out time on your calendar to really dive into contextualizing your curriculum or plan ahead for what you will be teaching.

Don't continue to the next page until your scheduled time is here.

Let's practice the skills of contextualizing!

Pull up the message you are teaching next, and run it through some of these filters:

How would you teach this content in . . .

> a room of one middle schooler and four volunteers?
>
> a room of 40 with a majority of middle schoolers who are unchurched?
>
> a room full of a majority of eighth-grade ladies who have grown up in church?
>
> a room full of fifth- to eighth-graders combined?
>
> your two environments (whatever they are)?
>
> your specific students after a natural disaster occurred in your town?

What about this specific talk that you are planning to give needs to be contextualized? (Go back and review the list of questions that can serve as a contextualization filter.)

_____

_____

_____

_____

_____

_____

_____

WRITE THE CONTENT

So, you know the topic you're teaching, and you're ready to start planning what you're going to say. We'll talk more later about the process of how you prepare to deliver your talk, but the first step? Actually writing the content.

Now before we jump in, I have to share one of the best lessons I have learned from people much smarter than me. I completed an Oratium Masterclass on Advanced Messaging Design and Delivery and it was FIRE. After two degrees in Education and 13+ years in the trenches, I sat there feeling like, "Wow, I still have so much to learn about communicating." My biggest takeaway from this Masterclass was the importance of understanding and aligning with how people process information—particularly when it's being spoken. According to brain science research, people process and learn sequentially. This is especially true for middle schoolers. Sequence creates context. Chapter Eight doesn't make sense without Chapter Six, which means the way we structure our message is critical. The information must flow in a logical and linear way because people get lost easily when exposed to new material. We could prepare the best sermon of our lives, but if it's not in the correct sequence with how a middle schooler processes the information, they will miss it.[36]

Knowing that, there are five things that the structure for a talk to middle schoolers should always include:

1. Introduction
2. Tension
3. Truth
4. Application
5. Landing

Now, you might not call it this, or you might do this in a different way. There are a ton of different ways to structure a talk.

In their book *Communicating for a Change*, Andy Stanley and Lane Jones suggest how to structure a talk that walks someone through the introduction of information to application for life change.[37] It looks like this:

ENGAGE	**ME** Orientation	**What** do you want them to **know**?	Topic Introduction
	WE Identification	**Why** do you want them to **know** it?	Tension Identification
INVOLVE	**GOD** Illumination	What does **God** have to say about it?	Tension Resolution
CHALLENGE	**YOU** Application	**What** do you want them to **do**?	Tension Reconciliation
	WE Inspiration	**Why** do you want them to **do** it?	Bottom Line

LIFE CHANGE

At Orange, we've adapted this structure to work best for communicating specifically to middle schoolers. It's the structure I've seen great communicators follow to be the most effective in allowing middle schoolers to process and apply the information they are being taught.

INTRODUCTION

The introduction is a great time to connect with the students in the room. When they know you like them and care about them, they will be more inclined to listen to what you have to say. Here, you might ask them a question and allow them to respond to you in real-time, or tell a personal story that relates to the topic you're talking about so they can get a glimpse into your life. The goal in this section is to not only establish connection and capture their attention, but to also begin to build trust right from the start. When they trust you, they'll be more likely to (try to) stay engaged for the remainder of your talk.

The introduction might sound something like . . .

⇨ "What's up, friends! My name is Ashley, and I am so excited to hang out with my favorite people on the entire planet this morning. Turn to the person next to you and say, 'You are one of my favorite people on the planet.'"

⇨ "Before we do anything else, I need your help with something . . . (Invite them to vote, stand up if _____, ask for volunteers, make a call back to something that happened right before your message started, etc.)"

⇨ Share a time from your own life that illustrates _____. Then ask, "Can you relate?"

TENSION

The tension you create in your message will help a middle schooler understand why they should even care about what you're talking about. It points out something the middle schooler is already feeling or already asking, even if they might not be aware they are feeling or asking it. The tension does not resolve that feeling or give answers, though. It should leave them on the edge of their seat waiting in anticipation to find out the answer. When building tension, it's important to remember that the tensions you're experiencing and the questions you're asking as an adult are not the same tensions that a middle schooler is experiencing. They aren't even the same tensions that a high schooler is feeling! This is why it's important to have a "go-to" team of middle schoolers you can ask questions to as you wrestle with the tension you will use in your talk.

The tension might start off sounding something like . . .

⇨ "Have you ever felt . . . ?"
⇨ "Why is it that . . . ?"
⇨ "Think about a time when you were told you were too _____ to do something . . ."
⇨ "Maybe this isn't something you think about very often, or maybe you can't stop thinking about it . . ."
⇨ "How are you supposed to know . . . ?"
⇨ "Maybe you think about it in a totally different way . . ."
⇨ "If you've ever asked . . ."

TRUTH

Once you've created and built the tension, you also want them to be wondering what God has to say about it. This is where you'll bring in the Scripture. This section breaks down the truth in a simple and effective way.

As you break down the truth, you'll want to introduce your main point, or the bottom line, of your message before moving on to the next section. If you practice giving your message to somebody and they can't summarize in one sentence what you talked about, you don't have a bottom line, and you don't have one clear idea.

The truth might sound something like . . .

⇨ "The good news is, we aren't the first people in history to ask these types of questions. In fact, there was a guy named John who walked this planet at the same time Jesus did, and he had a lot to say about this very thing."

⇨ "Before I tell you what Abraham said, we need to understand what is going on in this situation . . ."

⇨ "Take a look at what Paul said to Timothy . . ."

⇨ "When Matthew uses the word _____, what he means is _____."

⇨ "If there is anything I want you to remember when you walk out of here it is this: (hit the bottom line)."

APPLICATION

Now that they've experienced the tension you've created around what you're teaching, and they've heard what God has to say about it, what do you want your listeners to do with it? The application is where you'll give them clear steps they can take to apply that truth to their own lives. Remember, the way each person applies that truth may look different. **The goal isn't simply to deliver information. It's for them to apply the information they've learned.** When a middle schooler is able to use what they've learned, they'll be more likely to retain that information later.

The application might sound something like . . .

⇨ "If you are sitting there thinking, 'All of this sounds great, but what does it actually have to do with my life?' Great question. Here's how . . ."

⇨ "If this sounds like the kind of thing you are interested in, I want to challenge you with three things . . ."

⇨ "First, ask yourself if you really *do* trust God. Second, take one step to start acting like God is with you in the middle of all of this. Maybe that step looks like . . . Third, be brave enough to talk about it with people you trust."

LANDING

This is the wrap-up and where your bottom line, big idea, or sticky statement is repeated. The landing is where you cast vision for any small group or conversation time that follows your talk and where you help them imagine what life could be like if they lived this truth out. You might also land your talk by asking a question (or using another cue) for your middle schoolers to think about as they transition into whatever comes next.

The landing might sound something like . . .

⇨ "Can you imagine how your friend group, your school, this youth group would be different if we all actually did these things together?"

⇨ "So, remember, **[insert bottom line]**. You can be part of what God is doing to make the world better. And that can start today, with your small group! Small group is a great place to not only talk about our biggest questions about purpose, but to help each other figure out better answers, and figure out what role you can play in God's story today. I can't wait to hear how you encourage each other to do just that this week!"

⇨ "Let's commit to being a group of middle schoolers who know that **[insert bottom line]**. And because it matters so much, it's important that we keep talking about it together as we figure it out."

⇨ "As you head to small group, I want you to start thinking about this question . . ."

Great communicators include these (or something like them) in every talk, and are creative in how they do so.

If you want to see a copy of this kind of talk in action, go to tryorangefree.com to get a free sermon sample in this format.

Reflect & Contextualize

Pull up a past talk you have given. Read it, listen to it, or watch it.

While doing so, identify the Introduction, Tension, Truth, Application, and Landing. Rate yourself and make notes on how you can improve for next time!

INTRODUCTION

1   2   3   4   5

What was good?

_____

_____

What was clear?

_____

_____

What would you do differently?

_____

_____

TENSION

1 — 2 — 3 — 4 — 5

What was good?

_____
_____

What was clear?

_____
_____

What would you do differently?

_____
_____

TRUTH

1 — 2 — 3 — 4 — 5

What was good?

_____
_____

What was clear?

_____
_____

What would you do differently?

_____
_____

APPLICATION

1   2   3   4   5

What was good?

_____

_____

What was clear?

_____

_____

What would you do differently?

_____

_____

LANDING

1   2   3   4   5

What was good?

_____

_____

What was clear?

_____

_____

What would you do differently?

_____

_____

When writing your content, which part is hardest for you to prepare?

_____

_____

_____

_____

When giving a talk, which part is the hardest for you to deliver?

_____

_____

_____

_____

What is your favorite way to outline a message or talk?

_____

_____

_____

_____

_____

DO SOMETHING INTERACTIVE

WHY?

As an Education major, we talked a lot about the importance of differentiated instruction and often debated about learning style theories.

> **Differentiated instruction:** the process of identifying students' individual learning strengths, needs, and interests and adapting lessons to match them.[40]

> **Learning styles:** the idea that people learn in different ways.

Whether we realize it or not, the ideas of differentiated instruction and theories of learning styles are the foundational reason why we, as communicators to middle schoolers, use so much creativity in our delivery.

It's why we engage students with visuals, pictures, videos, and object lessons.
It's why we tell stories, use props, and give fill-in-the-blanks on note pages.
It's why we invite testimonies to be shared and organize problem-solving scenarios.
It's why we make students stand up and respond halfway through the lesson.

We do this because when we incorporate a diverse approach in communicating, we have a better chance of sharing the most important message on the planet—the Good News of Jesus—in a way that offers variety for every kid in the room.

Nobody modeled and demonstrated teaching in a way the audience would understand better than Jesus Himself. He was the King (literally) of using interactive elements in His teaching. Jesus knew exactly who He was talking to. He always used the perfect illustrations, asked the perfect questions, or told the perfect story to reach the people He was talking to. Jesus used things like mustard seeds, coins, sheep, stories, illustrations, and so much more to support His teaching—all of which appealed to different people, with different life experiences, who needed to hear truth in a very specific way.

UNDERSTAND LEARNING STYLES

There are several different theories when it comes to learning styles, all of which offer a different breakdown of learning styles. I appreciate them all for various reasons, but for the purpose of this book, we will briefly unpack one of the more common theories developed by Neil Fleming that states there are four types of learners: visual, auditory, reading/writing, and kinesthetic:[39]

Visual

Some of us learn best **visually**. Seeing is learning. These learners need to see a demonstration, a skit, a drawing, or a picture. Visual learners remember faces but forget names. They remember landmarks but not street names. They are distracted by movement or noise. When it can't be seen, descriptions help them to visualize a new concept in their heads as they are learning it.

Auditory

Others learn best by having the communicator verbally give instructions or content. These learners are called **auditory** learners. They enjoy dialogues and discussions, prefer audiobooks to physical books, and often remember names but forget faces. Auditory learners problem-solve best by talking it out.

Reading/Writing

Some learn best through **reading and writing**. They prefer to take in information that is displayed using words. They love words, words, and more words. They prefer to make lists, read textbooks and their Bible, take notes, and re-write their notes. They love worksheets and handouts, and they enjoy creating presentations. Rather than watch someone perform the task, they would rather read about how to perform the task in a book. This type of learner is one of the reasons we create slideshows with the main points displayed on the screen.

Kinesthetic

Lastly, some learners are **kinesthetic** learners. That means they need to move their bodies to learn, and absorb the most when they are involved in some type of activity. They typically have high energy levels. They lose much of what was said during the message, as they prefer hands-on learning and whole-body learning, rather than sitting and listening. Kinesthetic learners excel by completing projects, demonstrations, and labs.

Research has also shown us that regardless of dominant learning style, the more senses we engage, and the more variety we use in our teaching, the better chance we have at understanding what we are being taught. This is where differentiated instruction comes into play. The value of understanding how people learn is to challenge yourself as a communicator to think about how varied your teaching is. To learn more about *how* to differentiate your teaching, keep reading.

Remember, the goal of learning isn't just to understand new information. The goal is to do something with what we learn so we can retain it. We don't teach just to understand—we teach for application, for life transformation, and for change.

My favorite teacher on the planet was my history teacher, Mr. Rosati. Mr. Rosati was a master at differentiated instruction. I never even felt like I was in a classroom learning about what some would consider "boring" history. He made everything fun, engaging, and exciting. He would use different accents, sound effects, and visuals. He would act things out and include us in the skits. He would put his desk chair on top of his desk and tell us stories. He would climb into the drop ceiling and teach from above us. He didn't want to just tell us about history—he wanted us to feel it and experience it. We laughed so hard at times (especially when someone drew a huge "rocket ship" across the world map). He had a nickname for everyone in the room, and when he said it, the class would respond. He would invite guest speakers into the classroom unexpectedly. Mr. Rosati understood the value of engaging all senses and all learning styles. I think that's why I remember him the most. I remember thinking, "I want to teach like Mr. Rosati. He made learning so fun, and so easy, and he made me want to know more."

What if that's how we presented faith to this generation of middle schoolers?

Knowing and remembering that everyone has different learning styles is really important in planning the pieces of your talk. Naturally, we default toward communicating in the way we prefer to learn, or communicating in the only way that has been modeled for us. But **what if we were able to leverage every learning style in our delivery, so we reach every middle schooler in the room?**

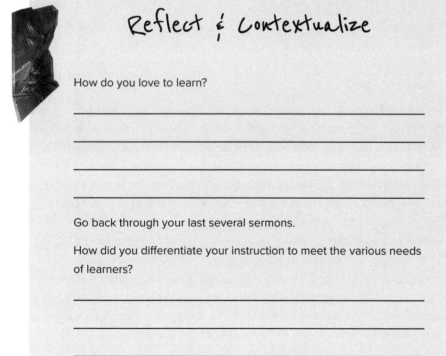

Reflect & Contextualize

How do you love to learn?

_____

_____

_____

_____

Go back through your last several sermons.

How did you differentiate your instruction to meet the various needs of learners?

_____

_____

_____

_____

Reflect & Contextualize

Brainstorm different ways to engage each of the learning styles when teaching faith concepts:

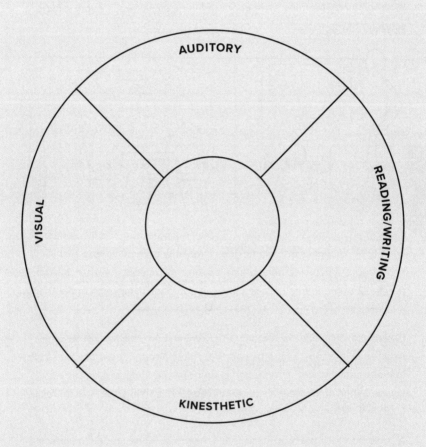

UNDERSTAND YOUR APPROACH

In my undergraduate work in School Health Education, we talked a lot about the difference between the "sage on the stage" versus the "guide on the side" approach to teaching.[40] This is especially relevant when it comes to teaching the physical, mental, social, emotional, and spiritual aspects of wellness. Why? Well, a kid's health needs to be personalized. Faith works kind of like that too.

SAGE ON THE STAGE   **GUIDE ON THE SIDE**

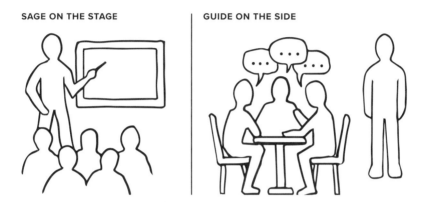

A "sage on the stage" means you, as the communicator, are the central figure who knows all the things, does a majority of the talking, transmits the knowledge, fills the learners' brains, so they can later regurgitate it when needed. For the learner, this is a passive approach to learning rather than an active one.

However, what we know about learning is that knowledge must be constructed and reconstructed by each individual through the process of trying to make sense of new information in terms of what that person already knows. When students are actively engaged in learning, they are more likely to retain information and apply it to their lives.

A "guide on the side" approach to teaching places the student as the central figure, actively participating in the learning process. The communicator is still responsible for presenting the information but does so in a way that leaves room for the students to interact with it. It's a shift from **transmission of information** to **construction of meaning** as middle schoolers work to make new, and often abstract, concepts concrete.

MAKE THE ABSTRACT CONCRETE

As we said in Chapter 1, middle schoolers are moving away from the concrete thinking they utilized during childhood, and they are beginning to think more abstractly. Abstract concepts are sometimes difficult for middle schoolers to grasp if they don't have anything concrete to anchor those concepts to because abstract thinking needs to be strengthened and developed. Like we said before, it is like a muscle that you gain the ability to use during puberty. We, as leaders, get to help them flex that muscle. And one way we can do that is by making abstract concepts concrete through interactive learning.

> **Interactive Learning:** any method of teaching middle schoolers that allows them to engage with you or each other in a creative way that invites feedback or engages more of their senses beyond seeing and hearing.

When a middle schooler is able to interact with something in their physical environment that explains or connects with the abstract truth you're trying to teach, it will make more sense to them and help them retain the information.

And of course, there is a big difference between comprehension and retention.

> **Comprehension:** understanding something fully.

> **Retention:** remembering information to be able to recall it later in the learning process.

When you comprehend information, you are simply taking in the information you are hearing. But in order for the information to stick, you need to interact with it and do something memorable with it.[41] This is true for middle schoolers, but it's also true for adults.

"

Discover a process or create a process that works for you, but whatever you do, trust the process. Trust the work of the Spirit in the process not just to come up with a good talk, but to do a refining work in you through the process. That is a process worth trusting."

—Vivi Diaz

JOB	LOCATION	EXPERIENCE
Next Gen Manager at Sandals Church	Riverside, CA, USA	8+ years of experience communicating to middle schoolers

Learn more about how Vivi prepares to communicate on page 236

HOW TO ENCOURAGE INTERACTION

So how do we help middle schoolers interact with what we teach in a memorable way so that they'll retain it?

1. Plan for them to talk.

Plan for them to talk out loud.

Give them permission to speak and to speak loudly. Ask them to shout or repeat something you've said. When they use their voices to interact with what you are teaching, they are more likely to remember it.

⇨ Have them make a noise on the count of three
   (this could be cheesy, but it's all in the delivery).
⇨ Have them cheer for something.
⇨ Have them do something to make noise in the room.
⇨ Have them read something out loud with you.

Plan for them to talk to each other.

I know, I know . . . you may be thinking, "I picked up this book to figure out how to get them to STOP talking to each other during my message." But here's my experience: If you plan for them to talk and be silly, and if you show them that you aren't afraid of them interacting with you, or each other, it's easier to pull them back in when you want their attention again. In fact, you may not even need to ask for it. Sometimes (and only sometimes), they will give you their attention back once you start talking because you demonstrated to them that you are taking turns in listening to each other. They'll be more likely to want to know what you're going to do or say next because they are engaged and invested.

So, think about cueing your middle schoolers to have conversations right where they are sitting. No matter if you call them "turn and tells," "turn and talks," or "forced fellowship," throw out a question for discussion and then give them one or two minutes to turn to the person next to them and talk about it.

⇨ "Turn and tell the person next to you . . ."
⇨ "Turn and ask the person sitting next to you if . . ."
⇨ "Sit in your small groups and answer this question . . ."

Plan for them to talk to you.

One of the quickest ways to take down any barrier between an upfront communicator and a room full of middle schoolers is to give them permission to speak directly to you.

⇨ Ask a question and on the count of three have them all shout their answers at you (you won't hear a thing, but they will feel heard). This tool is an excellent way to keep students engaged and to re-engage students who might have tuned out for a second. It also helps students connect to you personally, even if everyone in the room is also shouting along with them.

I was teaching in the middle school ministry at my local church, and I was explaining to the room that because I had just moved to Atlanta, I didn't know the cool places to eat or visit in the area. As you probably already know, middle schoolers love to be experts on things, and they love when you ask for their advice. So, of course, I asked for their advice. I said, "I'm brand-new to the area, and on the count of three, I want you to yell out a place I need to visit, or a place I need to eat." I have learned over the years, when I invite everyone to respond at the same time, I try to listen for just one answer to comment on and connect with. This time, a boy in the front row screamed "STARBUCKS!!!!" at the top of his lungs. And he wasn't joking. I love middle schoolers. I thanked him for the suggestion and told him I would definitely check it out.

2. Plan to use activities.

The basic idea is this: Create opportunities that allow some, or all, of your students to move around and participate in something that sets up or connects to the truth you are trying to communicate.

⇨ Play a few rounds of "Either/Or" during your introduction, and have students move to the side of the room that represents their choice between two options.
⇨ Have students answer a few questions by sitting down or standing up to show you their answer.

When you plan to use activities, chances are some of those activities might involve bringing a student up on stage (or to the front of the room) with you. Keep in mind that middle schoolers are incredibly insecure about what is happening to their bodies. So, if you are trying to get a middle schooler to do something in front of their peers and they resist, there is probably a physical explanation for it. Sweat stains. Period leakage. The wrong bra. A spontaneous erection. Gas. Food in their braces. Acne. Though it's all normal, it feels isolating to them, and the last thing they want to do is stand in front of their peers. So don't push them.

3. Plan to use props.

These are physical objects or demonstrations you utilize while you communicate. Props are especially helpful when you are teaching a narrative from Scripture! It's also a helpful cue for students. When they see that object in the future, they may think about the truth they learned that day.

Some examples might be using:

⇨ life-size cardboard cutouts to represent interacting with people when telling a story from the Bible.

⇨ a genie lamp to represent how sometimes, we can treat praying to God kind of like a genie who can grant us our three wishes.

⇨ a jar full of hundreds of pieces of candy to represent how many times God forgives us when we mess up.

⇨ a mirror to represent what it means to reflect the image of God.

⇨ a compass to represent making wise decisions.

Remember, just because you have seen a certain illustration a hundred times doesn't mean your students have. Sometimes, props or illustrations that feel overdone to adults are brand-new to teenagers, especially those who are new to the church world.

4. Plan to use technology.

If we want faith to feel important to a generation of middle schoolers, we need to be interacting with faith in the places that are important to them. And for this generation of middle schoolers, that is in the world of technology.

I realize not all communities have equal cellular service or high-speed Internet.

I realize not all middle schoolers have cell phones.

I realize not all church families have access to technology.

I realize not all parents are comfortable with their kid interacting with the latest social media platforms or apps.

Taking all of that into consideration, I still think using technology is a good thing when possible, appropriate, and accessible.

If they are interacting with some form of technology at school, at home, with their friends, and in the shows they watch, then we as the Church need to be speaking the same language so we don't come across as ancient and outdated. Plus, using technology is a great way to meet the needs of a variety of learning styles in the room.

You might use websites or apps to do live polls, host live Q&A's, prepare interactive slideshows, or display photos on the screen as you talk. You might be able to throw it to a clip from a well-known movie to illustrate something you are talking about, or press play on the most perfect song at the most perfect moment. You may be able to Zoom someone in from across the world and have a conversation, or pull up a clip of a kitten when someone needs cheering up. Or you might have them follow along with reading the Scripture you're teaching using a Bible app on their phones (if they have them). You might even encourage them to use social media, if they're on social media, to further engage with the topic.

BE STRATEGIC

When planning to do something interactive, be strategic about where that piece fits into the overall message. When you are speaking to middle schoolers, you should do something interactive in every single one of your talks. But here's the thing: Don't try to do something interactive in a place where it will distract from the point you're trying to make, and don't do it if it's unclear. If you have to spend too much time explaining your interactive, or if it derails your talk, don't do it. **An interactive element should help you make your point, not complicate it.**

It's easy to skip including interactives as you prepare the pieces, because these can oftentimes be areas that feel like we lose control of the room and our students. The truth is we might, but I think the risk is worth it. The more we try it, the more we will learn how to lead them through these moments and actually make it to the other side. In my experience, the less we talk formally about rules, and the more we give them opportunities to engage in different ways throughout our talk, the better I have seen middle schoolers behave. They need structure, but they don't love being told what to do or what not to do. So, when we approach interactive opportunities throughout our talk more like a space where they can be free, we let them know we aren't intimidated by their talking. Keep in mind that **rules about talking don't necessarily mean we'll see better behavior.** We'll talk about that more in a bit.

Planning the interactive elements during your talk starts way before you have a message ready to go. There are stories and interactive ideas everywhere. Like my pastor, mentor, and friend, Jeff Henderson, says, "Be preparing for your talk every day, in every encounter." When you do that, you constantly have a collection of ideas and illustrations and stories to pull from when you are planning the interactive pieces of your talk.

I was talking to a youth worker whose pastor was in a bank during a robbery, but the pastor didn't know it because they were on their phone the whole time. Keep your eyes up so you don't miss your next bank robbery story or inspiration for an interactive.

I do this for my personal social media and for middle school ministry. I am constantly taking pictures of things, or saving videos I find online, or writing down conversations with people that could work in a message one day—even if I don't have a particular talk in mind for it yet. My friends will tell you this. I'll be on a hike with them and start taking pictures of random things, and they will know, "Oh, she's collecting ideas again!"

Every time you teach a middle schooler, **do something interactive.** Even when it requires a little more time and a little more creative energy. When we do, we help middle schoolers discover how the truth we are trying to communicate connects to their lives right now in a way they'll not only understand but remember.

Reflect & Contextualize

Ways to encourage interaction:

Plan for them to talk to each other.

Plan for them to talk to you.

Plan for them to talk in the room.

Use activities.

Use games.

Use props.

Use technology.

Use pictures.

Use videos.

Use apps.

Use music.

Which do you use the most? Put a star next to it.

Which idea would be a new one you are excited to try? Put an exclamation point next to it!

Which idea scares you the most? Put a question mark next to it.

Pick up your phone and open your photos.

Scroll through your last 100 photos.

Is there anything you photographed that could work as an illustration or interactive?

Write it down in the spaces below.

TELL STORIES

The best middle school communicators I know tell great stories—all different kinds of stories. **Stories help make the abstract concrete,** and they can help a middle schooler understand how an idea actually plays out in a real-life situation.

I think what makes using stories to illustrate truth to middle schoolers even more compelling is that Jesus Himself always used stories when He taught too.

WHY TELL STORIES?

Stories help someone **connect to a person.** That person, namely, is you. When you start your talk with a story, it helps you become human to them, and that is really important if you are going to communicate on their level.

Stories help **develop empathy.** When telling a story, we're helping middle school humans develop empathy toward others by understanding how they might have felt in a certain situation. We need to remember that middle schoolers don't think like adults, but they do *feel* like adults. When we can connect with middle schoolers emotionally, we've connected with them on their level.

Stories give kids a **bigger perspective.** As my friends Kristen Ivy and Reggie Joiner often talk about, "Stories over time move us to imagine a world beyond ourselves and help shape someone's perspective."[42] The stories we read and hear can connect us to the things that are important, making life fuller, faith deeper, and hope stronger.

Stories help a middle schooler **understand abstract concepts.** An engaging story can help them see how an abstract concept relates to something in their own life. It helps them personalize an idea and realize how much it matters for them, right where they are. When presented with something new, a lot of times, they need help connecting the dots. **Stories make ideas concrete.**

Stories help **keep their attention.** Middle schoolers love stories, and if we tell stories, they love us as a communicator—especially if we tell an engaging story well.

SELECT A PERSONAL STORY

The first step to telling a personal story?
Select the point you want to illustrate, not the story you want to tell.

I've seen so many speakers tell a story because . . .

It's funny.
It's entertaining.
They like telling it.

However, if it doesn't help your students connect with the main point of your talk, it isn't helpful. It's just a time-filler. Instead of beginning with, "What story do I want to tell?" write your entire talk without it. Then ask, "What point is the most difficult to comprehend? Where do I need a narrative or an illustration?" Then, determine which story you already have that will do the job best.

When thinking about which story would be a great story to illustrate a point in your talk, consider your audience. Remember that they are not all guys, and they are not all girls. They are not all athletes, and they are not all artists. Keep in mind that your examples can't always be about the things you love. The best stories and examples are ones that fit the whole audience, where everyone can relate to something at one point in the story.

Sometimes, the best stories you can tell are stories from when you were in middle school. Sometimes. It shows them that you can relate because you were also a middle schooler at one point in time. It communicates to them that what they are going through is normal. It reminds them that they are not the only one struggling with something or the only one asking that question. And there is a good chance they will be able to relate to your story. Those are all positive things about sharing a story from when you were in middle school. But the downside of telling a story from when you were in middle school? It might make you sound really old. That tension you were feeling, or the technology you're talking about, might not even be a thing anymore. They might not be able to translate what the equivalent is for them, so they might not relate at all. So, be selective of the stories from middle school that you share.

For any story you share, it's important to consider the experiences of your audience as they are listening to your story. For example, sharing about a time when you were frustrated you only had five pairs of shoes to choose from in middle school might disconnect you immediately from the kid whose family could not afford new shoes for the entirety of middle school. Be cautious when sharing stories that include privilege, context, or information that your audience doesn't share. In doing so, you may actually disconnect from them rather than form a deeper connection.

The stories you share don't always have to be from when you were in middle school. They can be a story about something that happened this week. The great thing about telling a story that happened recently is you have a chance to show them, as an adult, that your faith is still growing. It shows them that you are still figuring it out. That you haven't arrived yet. That God can show up in everyday life. That faith is exciting, and it can still surprise you after so many years.

The tricky part will be that you will need to do some extra work. You'll need to break the story down for them. Does that tension you experienced this week translate to the same tension they are also experiencing as a middle schooler? Do they care about that? You'll want to connect the dots of what that story that happened this week in your life has to do with their life as a middle schooler. You will also need to discern if what you are sharing about your week is developmentally appropriate for an 11-year-old to hear.

Another important thing about stories is that your stories should be (mostly) true. I make it a policy to never lie in front of middle schoolers. Because they can figure out when someone is faking it faster than anyone else can. So, always base your stories in truth. You may skip some points or place extra emphasis on some points, but at the end of the day, **to tell a great story, tell a true story.**

It doesn't have to be this amazing, crazy story to be a great illustration. If you can help them connect to the emotion of it—if you can connect to something they've actually felt—you've used the story well.

Sometimes, this might be telling a story of personal failure, or when you've messed up, to illustrate a point. Stories of failure or mistakes, and what you've learned in the process, can be really helpful if it supports the point you're trying to make.

One of my favorite things about sharing stories of failure is these types of stories also help middle schoolers understand that just because you are on a stage speaking to them, you aren't perfect and you may have actually made some of the same mistakes they have made, which just makes you more relatable.

But the truth is, you don't always have to share stories of failure. You might have gotten it right sometimes! It makes a great story to talk about how you might have won in a specific area or situation.

PREPARE YOUR PERSONAL STORY

Once you know which story you're going to tell, first figure out what you want to say. Identify what the main point, or the goal, of your story is. How is your story going to help make the abstract concept you're talking about more concrete? Or how will your story help your audience really feel the tension you're about to set up?

Next, think about the points you want to make, the points you want to make sure are clear, the things you need to speed by, and the things you need to spend time on.

In any personal story you tell, you'll want to spend time on the tension. You want them to feel that tension, as if they were experiencing what happened in the story themselves. Spend some time there, pause, let them feel it. Because that's the tension that's going to make them wonder what God has to say about it. It's going to make them think about how they would answer the questions they are wrestling with. So please don't hurry past the tension.

Then, ask yourself: Is this story helpful for them, right now, as middle schoolers? Make sure that the point you are trying to make with your story is helpful and something that is relevant to their lives now.

Now that you know what you're going to say, plan how you'll transition into the story and how you'll transition out of the story. Besides the main point of your story, these are the two most important pieces. Like we'll talk about in a bit, the transitions are where you'll bring your middle schoolers along with you or where you'll lose them in the shuffle. So, know how you're getting into the story and how you're transitioning out of it.

In fact, that was one of the pieces of advice Danielle Strickland gave me at the Women's Speaker Collective. Instead of telling the room I was about to tell a story, she encouraged me to just start the story and invite them into it.

I started my story like this:

"Today marks 10 years I have been serving in Ethiopia. I want to tell you a story about a time I was having dinner at my friend Yetim's house. She was making *shiro wot*, an Ethiopian staple. If you have never had it, imagine warm hummus with a lot of butter."

Instead, Danielle encouraged me to start like this:

"I was sitting in a mud house in Ethiopia. The floor was mud, the walls were mud, but it smelled like heaven. My friend, Yetim, was making *shiro wot*, an Ethiopian staple. If you have never had it, imagine warm hummus with a lot of butter." And then pause to let the entire room imagine that.

Do you see how that small tweak made the story more interesting right from the beginning? I think sometimes with middle schoolers, they need a cue that you are about to tell them a story, but sometimes stories are better told the way Danielle coached me. The good news is you get to decide which method is right for you and your students.

PRACTICE YOUR STORY

Now that the content of your story is ready to go . . . PRACTICE. Practice in front of someone else who doesn't already know the story. Ask them which parts of the story need more clarity, which parts were confusing, and which parts may not be helpful. Ask them what questions they still have after hearing your story. Make sure that the tension you set up was clear and they were able to feel that tension too. Once you've gathered feedback from that person, make any changes to your story that would be helpful for your middle schoolers.

And lastly, record yourself telling your story as you prepare. As you listen to it back, look for dead spots or places where you need to connect the dots. Look for anywhere you don't sound confident in what you're saying, or a detail you may have forgotten to include, or places you may need to either speed through faster or spend more time on.

The truth is this: Stories are powerful. They are an incredible tool to help you connect with your audience in a personal way. They can help you as the communicator become more relatable and more human when they are told in a way that is clear, broken down, and relevant to your audience. Yes, preparing a story takes time, thought, and practice to make sure it's a great story. But it will be worth every second when a middle schooler is able to see how God shows up in everyday life.

⇨ Decide what you want to say.
⇨ Outline the points you want to make.
⇨ Figure out what you need to speed by.
⇨ Highlight the things you need to spend time on.
⇨ Ask yourself: Is this helpful for them right now?
⇨ Plan the transition into the story and the transition out of the story.
⇨ Practice in front of someone who doesn't know the story.
⇨ Record yourself telling the story to listen for dead spots of places where you need to connect the dots.

Stories are also an opportunity to highlight and celebrate a student or leader in your ministry, or give another student or leader a chance to share their story with your audience. If you choose to have someone tell their story, make sure to help them prepare. How? The same way you would prepare your own story, except allow for more prep time since they are perhaps not used to sharing their story or used to speaking in front of people. Make sure they practice in front of you or at least send you a video of them practicing. That way, you can provide feedback on the words they speak and their delivery.

TELLING A STORY FROM THE BIBLE

Using stories in your talk doesn't only mean sharing personal stories, it's also telling stories found in the Bible and the overarching story of the Bible too. And the good news is that middle schoolers love stories, so storytelling is a tool and an art that can help Scripture come to life and become more meaningful.

But just like we are telling true stories about our own lives, remember you are also telling stories about real people in the Bible, not fictional characters. Using the word "story" or "character" when referencing the Bible can be confusing.

When telling a story from the Bible (about real people), context also matters a whole lot. We should never talk about a verse of Scripture without giving them context of where it happened in the Bible, or where it happened within the bigger story of the Bible.

When we read the Bible, and help middle schoolers learn to read the Bible, it's not only important to read the words that were written but to also find out the "why" behind them. The more we learn about the background information, the more we can understand exactly why the author uses specific words, phrases, or examples that may seem strange to us today.

A study Bible offers not only the biblical text but notes about what's going on behind-the-scenes, or an explanation of what something means to provide more context. There may be a page included before the start of each book that gives a little bit of the background on the author, as well as the time period in which it was written. Learning more about the author helps us know why they may have had a certain perspective, and learning about the time period gives us background on what other things were going on in that specific area at the time.

When we read something that seems a little bit strange to us, it's always important to look at the context. One helpful way to do this is to use the 5 W's:

WHO, WHAT, WHEN, WHERE, AND WHY?

When we answer these questions, it helps us to break down what we're reading.

WHO: Who wrote this book? Do we know what they did, who they were, and where they were from?

WHAT: Do we know exactly what the author was trying to say? Have we read the verses before and after to know what else is being said?

WHEN: When was this written? What else was going on at this time in history? What was life like for people back when this was written?

WHERE: Where is this taking place? Do we know anything about the people who lived there?

WHY: Why did the author feel the need to write this? Why did they use specific words or phrases?

Context brings clarity to help all of us, not just middle schoolers, understand the big picture story of the Bible.

At the Women's Speaker Collective Bootcamp, Danielle Strickland led us through an exercise of preparing to tell a story from Scripture by thinking through the different perspectives present in the story. Our small group was assigned to read Mark 5:21-43. Each person was assigned a different perspective and had to give a one-minute presentation of thoughts from that perspective. I was assigned "the crowd." So here I am reading about the woman who bled for 12 years, trying to picture what everyone in the crowd must have been thinking. Wow. Once everyone at my table shared from the perspective they read from, I was blown away by the depth that this exercise brought. It brought this story to life in a whole new way. It made me think through so many of my students, things I had never thought about before, and how I could share this story in a way that made them feel seen and included in it. I thought this exercise was an excellent way to prepare to tell a story from Scripture. We have to get better at reading Scripture with people who have a different perspective than us because it allows us to think of questions we would have never thought to ask.

One of the best ways to grow as a communicator is to become a great storyteller. Whether you tell a story from your own life, tell someone else's story, or tell the story of an event in history, you have the opportunity to make the abstract concrete and real for a middle schooler. Relating to a story and personalizing it for themselves is key in helping a teenager develop a faith of their own. So, every time you teach a middle schooler, **tell stories.**

Reflect & Contextualize

What is one story from your own life that might help middle schoolers connect to you as a person?

_____

_____

_____

_____

_____

_____

_____

_____

_____

_____

What is one of your favorite stories from Scripture that might help middle schoolers connect with Jesus as a Person?

_____

_____

_____

_____

_____

Find that story in the Bible and answer the following . . .

Who? _____

_____

_____

What? _____

_____

_____

When? _____

_____

Where? _____

_____

Why? _____

_____

_____

_____

Let's practice crafting your own personal story for middle schoolers. Think through how you would tell it, what you might leave out, and what you would emphasize.

Here are a few story prompts to get you thinking:

Have you ever succeeded at something you thought you'd fail at?

_____

_____

Think of a time you needed to forgive someone.

_____

_____

Describe a moment in your life when you felt overlooked.

_____

_____

Talk about a time you were overcome with joy.

_____

_____

Share about your most embarrassing moment in middle school.

_____

_____

Now, let's practice re-telling Bible stories and think through the lens of a different person's perspective (even if that person's words aren't recorded):

Jesus fed a crowd with five loaves of bread and two fish—Matthew 14:13-21 (from the perspective of another child in the crowd)

_____

_____

_____

_____

Jesus calmed the storm—Matthew 8:23-27 (from the perspective of the fishermen's friends when they heard what happened)

_____

_____

_____

_____

David defeated Goliath—1 Samuel 17:41-52 (from the perspective of David's brothers)

_____

_____

_____

_____

USE HUMOR

If you walk through the halls of any middle school, or sit on any middle school bus, or stand on the sidelines of any middle school soccer game, or jump on any FaceTime call that includes middle schoolers, it doesn't take much time to realize that middle schoolers love two things: they love to be funny and they love to laugh. In my opinion, middle schoolers are the most fun and the funniest people on the entire planet.

So, as a communicator, why not lean into that?

Use humor throughout your talk as a way to make them laugh and connect with them. When you make a middle schooler laugh, you begin to break down their walls. When you break down their walls, you help them open up to receive the truth you're about to share with them. Also, make sure to laugh at yourself as much as you make them laugh. Be careful to laugh with them, not at them.

Laughing with them, as a whole group, also creates a bond. Not only between you and the group, but between everyone in the group too. According to research, laughing with others signals our brain to release *endorphins*, the chemicals that make us feel good.[43] When endorphins are released in groups of people, it creates a sense of unity and safety among the group.

If you're anything like me, you struggle with humor too—because I am not a comedian. In fact, you might be the furthest thing from a comedian, and that's okay. You don't have to be a comedian in order to use humor and be funny with middle schoolers. Use the kind of humor that works for you.

There are a few things that are important to keep in mind when it comes to using humor with middle schoolers.

Be careful not to use humor when you're about to make a big point. This just distracts their focus, and you will have to work hard to bring them back. Humor is important. Just use it in the right places.

Be careful with sarcasm. Middle schoolers don't always grasp the concept of sarcasm. Because of the way their brains are developing, they sometimes have trouble deciding when you are being serious and when you are trying to be funny. They take a lot of what is said at face value.

Be careful with self-deprecating humor. Especially during the middle school phase when students are questioning so much of their own value and unique identities, it's important to show students that you can laugh at yourself and that you don't take yourself too seriously. If you want your middle schoolers to believe that they are made in the image of God, then you have to show them you believe you are also made in the image of God. Self-deprecating humor can easily undermine that, so be selective.

Be careful not to use humor at the expense of others—especially when it comes to embarrassing stories. Stay away from sharing stories that you'd be embarrassed by if you were the person it happened to. There are times when sharing an embarrassing (and funny!) story that happened to a friend or family member is a perfect illustration for a talk. As you prepare to share it, think through how you'll tell it in a way that honors the person in the story.

Keep in mind that humor also varies by culture. What's funny and acceptable in one culture may be totally inappropriate in another. Humor is also often bound by very powerful (unwritten) social rules. Depending on your context, or if you're communicating with middle schoolers from a different culture or context than yours, be mindful of using humor that may unintentionally cross a line. If you're not sure, run it by someone more familiar with that culture first, or play it safe by not including that line or that joke in your message.

Breaking down the walls with your middle schoolers can be challenging, but humor that's appropriate, concrete, and intentional can be a great tool to help you do that. So, remember, every time you teach a middle schooler, **use humor.**

Reflect & Contextualize

On a scale of 1-10, how easy do you find it to use humor in your messages?

O———O———O———O———O———O———O———O———O———O

1   2   3   4   5   6   7   8   9   10

What do you think a middle schooler would find funny?

_____

_____

_____

Think back through the last few messages you have given, and document anything that happened that you remember middle schoolers laughing at:

_____

_____

_____

Document anything that happened that YOU found funny, but your middle schoolers did not:

_____

_____

_____

Pause.

Text five volunteer small group leaders, or parents of middle schoolers, and ask them what their middle schoolers find funny. Document their input here:

_____

_____

_____

_____

_____

_____

_____

_____

Now, text 10 different middle schoolers, and ask them to send you the funniest meme, GIF, TikTok, or YouTube video they have seen lately. Document your observations here:

_____

_____

_____

_____

_____

_____

_____

_____

_____

_____

STRATEGICALLY PROGRAM

Ministry is way too difficult to not do it strategically, and ministry is way too important to not have a strategy. Doing strategic ministry means a lot of different things, but for the context of this book, let's say it means having the end in mind. It means knowing what's happening before you and what's happening after you in the flow of the program. That might look like small group time, a worship response, or the ending of the program.

Whatever that looks like in your context, it means thinking about the entirety of the program from start to finish. When you know the entire flow, you'll be set up to win, and you'll also be able to set up whatever is happening next to win too.

The next step in knowing where you are in the program is connecting where you are as the communicator to what's happened before and what is going to happen after you. If you are communicating after a student was just baptized, you might call back to that at some point in your talk. You might decide to directly address that student and publicly affirm them.

I make sure to view the bumper video ahead of time so I know what kind of energy it does or doesn't bring. If the bumper is serious and ends on a down beat, and then the lights come on, and I scream "HELLO!" at the top of my lungs, it has the potential to throw off everybody in the room.

If you follow a song that the band just played, encourage them with how they sounded, or talk about something you love about that song.

If something really funny happened when you were playing a game, acknowledge it and keep laughing about it.

Every time you teach a middle schooler, **strategically program.** When you do that, you're able to connect the pieces of the program for your middle schoolers, so they can make the jump to the next thing with you.

Reflect & Contextualize

Pull up Planning Center Online (or whatever platform your ministry uses for programming).

Scroll back through the last five service plans.

Did you strategically plan each transition in the program?

_____ No. Don't judge me.

_____ Ummm. Kind of?

_____ YES. It's written out.

In the notes of each program piece, take a few minutes and write out how you plan to transition from one thing to the next.

_____

_____

_____

_____

_____

_____

_____

_____

_____

YOU GOT THIS!

3. PREPARE YOUR DELIVERY

So, now you have your content. You've developed pieces you're going to use throughout your message.

Maybe you wrote it, or you edited it from a curriculum you downloaded. You know what you are teaching, but what exactly comes next? How do you go about preparing yourself to deliver the Good News to middle schoolers? Delivering a message to a gathering of adults is not the same as delivering a talk to a group of middle schoolers. That is why your preparation may also need to look different.

Before I go any further, I want to acknowledge that you may be preparing to deliver your talk to a combined group of middle and high school students. I encourage you to keep reading, but if you want to read more specifically on delivering to a combined environment, jump to page 216, and then come back!

In the last chapter, we talked about planning the pieces of your talk, such as your outline, props, stories, visuals, technology, interactives, etc. This typically comes before preparing your actual talk. However, depending on how you prepare, it might not happen in that order (like me). You might start with planning your pieces, but jump back and forth between the two once you've moved on to preparing your talk, and that's okay.

First, I am going to share how I prepare, but I realize you are not me. We don't have the same personality. We don't have the same strengths and weaknesses. You don't learn the same way I learn, which means how you prepare may look drastically different, and that is okay. The way I prepare is just one of many ways to prepare. You need to find what works for you. Chances are, that will be a process. It has taken me a lot of years to learn what works best for me.

At the end of this book, in a section called Bonus Content (page 224), I have invited some of my dear friends—who are all experts at communicating to middle schoolers—to share what works for them. Of course, there is no right or wrong way to prepare for a talk, but like we all have a learning style preference, we each have our preferred method.

If you are trying to figure out what works for you, I want to challenge you to first read through all of these different ways to prepare. Then, try some or all of these ways. In fact, you might need to try them out multiple times. As you do, you'll quickly learn what works best for you, what absolutely does not work for you, what's helpful, and what's not.

HOW I PREPARE

The very first thing I do when preparing to teach is read the entire series, if there is one, as many weeks ahead of time as possible. This is why using a curriculum is so helpful. I need to understand where we are going, where we are coming from, how not to step on the toes of the weeks that follow, and how to set up the following week. I always want enough time to feel it, not just know it. I spend at least four times the amount of time preparing for a talk as I do delivering it.

Once I know the direction of the talk, I need to move and pray about it. I am not a stay-in-one-place-and-talk-to-God kind of person. I ask God to show me what I can't see, to teach me what I don't understand, and I pray for the students, leaders, and parents on the other side of the message.

After I am in the headspace to begin preparing my talk (or contextualizing it if I am using curriculum), I create my slides. Even if I am not actually using slides during my talk, I always create them first to prepare. This is how I have been preparing talks since I started my career. I don't make my slides fancy. I am not a designer. I don't get caught up on how they look at this point. I just build the basics of the slides to visually lay my talk out because I need to see the full talk from beginning to end.

When I have created my slides, I copy and paste the pieces of my talk I have prepared onto multiple slides. This includes any pictures I plan to show, Scripture, words I plan to define, questions I plan to ask, video clips, etc.

When I've got all my pieces onto the slides, I put the slides in the order of how I initially think my message will flow. At this point, I start copying and pasting my notes into the notes section under each individual slide. I put as much information as I can about what I want to say about the content that is on that slide. If I plan to tell a story, I will note, "story about the squirrel." I don't write anything out word-for-word, except for my transitions. The last sentence on the note section of each slide is the exact line I am going to say to transition to the next slide. During this part of the process, I highlight any words or phrases on each slide that I plan to define and break down.

Then, I walk away from it for a few days. Time away helps me make sure that it makes sense logically. **I ask myself if every transition I have planned is specifically answering the question a middle schooler would be asking next in their head.**

Once I know the order of my talk is logical, I start deleting notes until I have just a few words to cue me.

Now starts the memorization portion of my prep. I want to first acknowledge that not everyone memorizes word-for-word scripts, including myself. I literally can't do that—my brain doesn't work that way. However, I do find it helpful to memorize my outline so I know the content well enough to adjust on the fly.

In order to memorize my outline, I memorize the order of my slides. I usually do this by going for a walk, working in my garden, or going for a drive while saying the order of the slides out loud. I need to be moving my body and active in order to remember something. If I sit and look at a computer screen, I will not remember it.

After memorizing the order of my slides, I start practicing the talk out loud. There is something very different about knowing your talk in your head and feeling it come out of your mouth. I've found that I can know my talk inside and out, but if I haven't practiced it out loud, it never delivers as well as I hoped. Using the voice memo feature on my phone, I record myself giving the talk. Then, I (painfully) listen to myself. I listen for dead spots, any places I seemed to get lost in what I was saying, or if I didn't connect any ideas well enough.

By now, I will have practiced the talk at least three full times.

Personally, I don't like using notes when I speak. I don't think it's wrong, but for me, notes can be distracting. So, I just let the slides remind me of what's coming next. If I have access to a screen with slides, and a preview monitor in the back, I prefer to have my current slide on the screen facing students, and my next slide visible on the monitor facing me.

So, I memorize what I want to talk about based on the slides. The only things I script out and memorize word-for-word is the introduction, each transition, and the landing of my talk.

When it's time to show up to the weekly program, I practice running through my transition statements with whoever is running my slides, if it's not me. This ensures they know the cue that I am using to move to the next slide without me having to say, "next slide, please" during my talk.

Lastly, I think it's important for you to know this: I have been doing this for almost 20 years, and I still never feel fully ready. I still get really nervous. Every single time. Honestly, I can never relate to people who say they never get nervous to speak. I pace back and forth and can feel my heart beat a little faster. If there's worship before I speak, I sing along with the music to drown out the voice of doubt with the voice of truth. I always breathe deeply before getting up to speak. I don't know if it's adrenaline, nerves, or my

"

If you feel nervous, make sure you allow yourself margin to eat a healthy meal before you speak and enough time to digest it! It keeps you grounded. If you are running from one thing to another without feeding your body something nutritious, it makes it hard to concentrate and be present and comfortable in your body. Give yourself extra time! Show up early so you are not stressed out getting things situated and feeling panicked. Give yourself the margin to handle anything that unexpectedly comes your way (like no Wi-Fi, tech problems, you forgot a teaching prop at home, etc.)."

—Gina Abbas

JOB	LOCATION	EXPERIENCE
Author and Speaker	Grand Rapids, MI, USA	20+ years of experience communicating to middle schoolers

Learn more about how Gina prepares to communicate on page 248

asthma flaring up from fog machines, but I have to take some deep breaths every time. Then, right before going on stage, I pray. I ask God to show up and speak through me—that I would get out of the way so instead of seeing me, people see the Spirit of God in me.

Again, this is not the right way to prepare—it's just what works for me. Maybe your prep process looks much different. In fact, reading through the preparation methods of others that we've included at the end of this book was fascinating to me. It also challenged me to experiment with a few new ideas in my own prep process. Whatever you do, don't miss the Bonus Content on page 224.

KEEP IT SHORT

Thanks to YouTube, TikTok, and Instagram Reels, the attention span of a middle schooler (or actually everyone) is getting shorter and shorter. Some say attention spans may be only eight seconds at this point.[44]

The average length of a YouTube video is 11 minutes and 42 seconds,[45] indicating the amount of time people can listen to a message is not much longer.

I don't love making a blanket statement about how long a talk should or shouldn't be, but I am asked this question consistently. I have often wondered if the total number of minutes isn't the best way to measure a talk. What if there is a better way?

One of the things we talked about at the Oratium Masterclass was that the people we are speaking to have a finite capacity to absorb information. We all process information with *working memory*, which happens in our frontal lobe.

Working Memory: a short-term memory process that keeps new information in mind as it accesses prior knowledge and makes connections.[48]

Our working memory is very limited. The person hearing information for the first time is assimilating the information and visual images, then relating it to their world in real time. This is hard, and it takes time and mental energy. Most of the time, we've been living with this content for weeks, and maybe years. Middle schoolers are processing it for the first time and in real time. When we overload them, they shut down.[47]

Short doesn't equal shallow.

The Gettysburg Address was fewer than 275 words, and it lasted just two to three minutes. President Abraham Lincoln wasn't even the main speaker, but his address is the only one that's remembered from that day.[48]

It will never be about the number of words we speak, but the power of the words we speak.

Anyone who has worked with middle schoolers for any length of time doesn't need to be convinced that it's hard to keep their attention.

I love what my friend Kurt Johnston wrote about in his book *Controlled Chaos* about the difference between attention span and interest span. He wrote, **"If you can increase their interest in what you have to say, you won't have trouble keeping their attention."**[49] I think this shift in focus has the potential to change the ability we have to connect with and relate to middle schoolers.

Nobody keeps the interest of a middle schooler like my dear friend Heather Flies, a veteran Junior High Pastor in Minnesota. I have had the honor of watching her communicate to middle schoolers a handful of times.

Heather happens to be one of the most engaging people I have ever met. Something I've noticed about her that sets her apart from others is her ability to make whomever she is talking to, no matter who they are, feel like they are the most interesting person on the planet.

Heather knows her students—like every single one of them. Maybe that's why she successfully engages her students for a solid 40 minutes. Heather is dynamic in every way. She incorporates humor, passion, and emotion to connect students to the information they are discussing. You see, Heather doesn't just talk at them, or over them; **she talks with them.** She plans time for students to interact with her and to interact with each other by asking questions and doing activities to anchor the truth of what she teaches to something tangible, and she has them immediately apply what they are learning. She is the definition of the guide-on-the-side approach we talked about in Chapter 2.

She knows every kid's name (cue the confetti), and after they share or participate, she gives them positive feedback and encouragement, which makes more students show interest in the topic.

Heather keeps their interest by helping them connect the dots between what they know to be true and what they are learning about God. She helps them correlate what God says and what that actually looks like in their life. She meets her students where they are but takes them on a journey and challenges them to be more. Heather believes that middle schoolers should be taken seriously and that they have something incredible to offer, and they know it. In fact, this is one of the reasons she can teach for 40 minutes—her students will follow her anywhere.

Before a teenager can know God, they may need to be known by an adult who knows God,[50] in the way that Heather knows her students. That's why, when it comes to middle schoolers, our goal as youth workers should be to aim for their interest rather than their attention.

Heather is an incredible example of how it is possible to teach longer than the middle school attention span by consistently engaging students and keeping their interest.

However, if you are teaching for 40 minutes, but you are NOT teaching in a way that captures their interest, which includes continually redirecting them, re-engaging them, and including time for discussion, I would venture to say you're probably facing some behavior issues in your group, and your students are probably not that interested in what you have to say.

Middle schoolers CAN focus their attention if they want to. I mean, have you ever seen a middle schooler sit and play Fortnite or Roblox for six hours straight? **While middle schoolers may display a short attention span, I think their interest span is much longer.** Like Kurt said best, **"Our objective is to increase their interest in the things of God. So, when you**

"

As a youth pastor, I wear a lot of hats, and honestly, I don't have 25 hours in a week to give. Of course, I don't want to short-change the process, but I've also never felt it necessary to give more than eight hours for message prep. It's never just one day. Often, it's a few hours over the course of a few days. I guess that might be the most important thing to communicate to you: do what works for you, within your wiring and your context!"

—Katie Edwards

JOB	LOCATION	EXPERIENCE
Student Ministries Pastor at Saddleback Church	Lake Forest, CA, USA	28+ years of experience communicating to middle schoolers

Learn more about how Katie prepares to communicate on page 228

increase their interest in what you have to say, you won't have trouble keeping their attention."[51]

If you or your volunteer leaders find yourselves continually shushing a room or repeatedly saying "shhh," or desperately trying to get middle schoolers to focus on what you are doing, you don't have a crowd control problem (teachers call this classroom management), you have an engagement opportunity. You have a clear signal that you need to re-engage them (not just control their behavior) and that it may be time for a group reset.

As I observe amazing middle school communicators, it seems consistently helpful to have a five-minute rule where the speaker commits to redirecting or recapturing their attention every five minutes. This is where the interactive elements we talked about in Chapter 2 come into play. Keep reading to find out HOW to do that!

Remember, our goal is not to deliver information. Our goal is for middle schoolers to carry that information when they leave. This only happens when we give them the opportunity to personalize, generate meaning, and integrate that information into their memories.

Maybe the best way to measure the length of a talk is by how long it takes to break down ONE concept or ONE sticky statement, rather than measuring it by the total number of minutes we speak. Sometimes it takes eight minutes to break down one concept and sometimes it takes 40, but I think we can all agree that the way you use the minutes matters.

Every time you teach a middle schooler, **keep it short.**

Here's the thing: A message that is eight minutes is even harder to prepare than a message that is 20, 30, or 40 minutes because every single word you say in that time has to matter. It requires more intentionality and practice to master this. And when you do, you'll give them the opportunity to digest bite-size pieces of information in a way they can actually apply to their everyday lives.

Reflect & Contextualize

What was the last TikTok or YouTube video you shared with a friend?

_____

_____

What drew you to it?

_____

_____

How long was it?

_____

_____

How long are your current messages to middle schoolers?

_____

_____

What do you find most challenging when trying to keep the attention
of middle schoolers?

_____

_____

_____

What are your go-to's to keep the attention/interest of middle schoolers?

_____

_____

What is something new you can try?

_____

_____

What are some things your students are interested in that you should learn more about?

_____

_____

Is there someone in your area who is really great at communicating to middle schoolers who you can observe?

A teacher?

A pastor?

A camp speaker?

Text them right now and schedule a time to observe them. When you do, write down what you learned that you can try to implement.

_____

_____

_____

_____

PLAN YOUR TRANSITIONS

Have you ever seen a snowmobile pulling a sled attached with a rope? Every turn has to be planned in advance. Why? When the snowmobile takes a quick turn, the sled takes a much wider turn and could potentially crash into the trees or bushes. It's not a great outcome for those on the sled, but this is often how we approach teaching middle schoolers. We only account for ourselves (the snowmobile) to make it around the turn to the next part of our talk. We don't always consider who is on the sled—our middle schoolers—and how long it may take them to recognize we are changing the subject or talking about something new. If we don't have a plan for them to make the turn with us, we could lose them. That's why . . .

We need a plan for transitions.

And by "transitions," I mean all transitions—the ones within your talk and also the transitions during programming. Transitions like . . .

- ⇨ the welcome into the game
- ⇨ the game into worship
- ⇨ worship into teaching
- ⇨ teaching to small groups

In each transition, you're either going to lose them or bring them with you.

If you live with a middle schooler or are related to one in your extended family or friend group, you will hear them ask these kinds of questions probably more times than you want them to:

"What are we doing today?"
"When are you going to the grocery store?"
"How long until we get there?"
"Are we doing anything fun this weekend?"
"What's for dinner?"
"When can I get my screens back?"
"Do I have to take a shower tonight?"
"When can I get a phone?"
"Do I have to?"

Middle schoolers are often thinking about what's next.

The next fun thing.
The next thing to avoid.
That thing they want next.

And when they don't know what's next,
the response is usually, "I am bored."

When we lose them in these transitions, they start talking to each other, touching each other, zoning out, throwing things at each other, or all of the above. You have to not only reset their attention, but you have to remind them what you are talking about all over again.

So how do we bring them with us? By using **consistent cues.**

> **Cue:** a thing said or done that signals to teenagers that something's about to begin or a transition is about to happen.

A cue during your programming might look like:

⇨ A countdown video means you're going to start programming.
⇨ A familiar greeting that students participate in signals the start of a game.
⇨ The lights going down and music coming on (or the band entering the stage) signals that you're about to start worship.
⇨ A bumper video can cue that you're starting your lesson.
⇨ A familiar line or question from stage cues them you're ending your lesson.
⇨ Walkout music will indicate that it's time for students to head to their small group.

You might tell them you're about to transition within your talk by saying something like:

⇨ "Maybe you've felt like _____ before . . . "
⇨ "The good news is we aren't the first people to feel this way . . ."
⇨ "One time, Jesus had a conversation with someone . . ."

⇨ "Here's how I know this is true . . ."

⇨ "This is why this is important . . ."

⇨ "You might be sitting there wondering . . ."

When we know where we're going next in our talk, we can bring them with us.

The best way to make sure you know where you're going? Memorize your transitions.

The best transitions I have observed answer the question middle schoolers are asking next in their head.

That's why it's helpful for me to memorize my introduction, every transition, and the closing when I am preparing my talks. I have an outline for everything else in between. When it comes to middle schoolers, the transition from one idea to the next is crucial. They need you to make it clear how the topic you are talking about first connects to what you are talking about next.

Every time you teach a middle schooler, **plan your transitions.** It's in the transitions that you have the opportunity to either bring them with you and engage them further, or lose them in the shuffle.

Reflect & Contextualize

Describe a time a transition was awkward or didn't go as planned.

_____

_____

_____

What ideas do you have for moving middle schoolers along with you as you deliver your talk?

_____

_____

_____

What is one part of your program where you struggle with transitions (for example, transitioning from worship to the game or from your talk to small groups)?

_____

_____

_____

What are three things you could try to make that transition smoother?

1. _____

2. _____

3. _____

USE VISUAL PIECES

We already know that some of our middle schoolers are visual learners, and because research has shown that appealing to more than one learning style—even if it's not your dominant—boosts learning,[52] we should incorporate visual pieces whenever possible.

This might look like . . .

⇨ displaying teaching slides on stage or in the front of the room.
⇨ having a monitor next to you as you teach to display words or graphics.
⇨ giving your students a handout or note page to write or doodle on as they listen to your message.
⇨ using a prop that makes an abstract concept more concrete.
⇨ showing a movie clip that illustrates what you're talking about.

HANDOUTS

Handouts and note pages can be beneficial in guiding middle schoolers in breaking down information. For some students, especially those who are reading/writing learners, taking notes or doodling can help them process what they are hearing. It doesn't mean they aren't listening.

Handouts or note pages can also be incredibly useful when they are passed out to your audience before you start speaking. That way, during your message, they are simply highlighting or jotting down what the information you're presenting them with actually means for them. Using handouts or note pages in this way can actually enhance the learning process and guide your audience in constructing meaning from what you are saying.

At the same time, handouts and note pages, especially fill-in-the-blanks, have the potential to be a distraction rather than an aid in the learning process because they don't boost engagement. Instead, they do the opposite, because your audience actually disengages while they're writing. While they are scribbling down notes of everything you are saying, or focusing on the one word they are missing for the fill-in-the-blank, they are focusing on what you are saying instead of what it actually means. This is where information gets lost, and the transfer of knowledge is lost too.[53]

Also, having to pause to wait for your audience to finish filling in the blank can be really annoying.

SLIDES

For many communicators, slides are an essential tool and a primary visual. They can also be a primary source of distraction if we don't use them well. If you use slides, here are a few things to keep in mind:

⇨ Each slide should have no more than 10 words.

⇨ If there is a word or phrase on your slide that you are directly addressing, defining, or pointing out, it should be highlighted, bolded, or in a different color than the rest of the text.

⇨ If you have a list to display, don't show everything in that list on the same slide so that it appears at the same time. People will read ahead instead of focusing on the point you're talking about in the list. Instead, if you have a list of three things, create three different slides, where each part of the list builds as you present the list. Highlight the point that you'll address on each slide.

⇨ If you highlight a word on a slide, make sure it is not highlighted when the next point pops up.

⇨ If you're giving a lot of information about a certain point, or using a long passage of Scripture that you want displayed, split the slide and make it build.

⇨ Use the minimal number of words possible on each slide. It's okay if it's not a complete sentence or thought.

⇨ If you are telling a story, show a picture or a short video from your story. Instead of saying, "I am going to tell you a story about my friend, Shem . . ." you can direct them to look at the screen and say, "Here's my friend, Shem. What you can't see in this picture is right behind Shem . . ." This helps your audience visualize the event or the person you're talking about, and it gives your students more of a glimpse into your life too!

If you've ever felt the pain of a slide mishap during your talk, you know this already: **There is a difference between planning (creating) your slides**

and preparing to use your slides. Here are a few things to think about when preparing after you've created the slides:

- ⇨ As you run through your talk with your slides, did anything trip you up?
- ⇨ Find the person who knows you and thinks the way you think. Ask them, "Do these slides make sense? What would you change to make them clearer?"
- ⇨ Make sure what you are talking about is what is on the screen.
- ⇨ If you are done talking about what's on the screen, and not ready to talk about what's on the next slide, just take the slide down so it is not distracting. It's okay to let the screen go dark.
- ⇨ Make sure you know your slides in case something happens with technology.
- ⇨ As you run through your talk, see if you skip anything when you are running through your slides. If you skip something, you might want to ask yourself if you really need that slide, or if you really need to make that point.

If you choose to use slides or a monitor next to you as you teach, make sure to interact with it while you're up there. Acting like it doesn't exist will only be a distraction instead of a support to the point you're trying to make. So, point to it. Walk over to it. Look at it. Motion toward it when you're talking about that specific point.

PROPS

While slides are important to many speakers (including me!), nothing on screen can keep their attention quite like an object in hand (refer back to page 102 in Chapter 2).

Some of the best speakers I know use . . .

- ⇨ paper shredders to talk about forgiveness.
- ⇨ rubber bands to talk about how shooting words at another person can seem fun but it can hurt.
- ⇨ cell phone chargers to describe the relationship between the Vine and branches.

⇨ "Hello My Name Is" stickers to talk about identity.

⇨ a campfire to talk about how you can feel close or far from God (be careful with fire!).

Every time you teach a middle schooler, **use visual pieces** that clearly and concisely support the point you're trying to make.

Reflect & Contextualize

What visual pieces are your favorite to use? Why?

_____

_____

_____

What visual pieces are your least favorite to use? Why?

_____

_____

_____

Pull up your latest slide deck (if you use slides). Run your slides through the bulleted list mentioned earlier.

What did you nail?

_____

_____

_____

What is one thing you want to improve next time you build a slide deck?

_____

_____

_____

4. ENGAGE YOUR STUDENTS

SHOW UP

Middle schoolers can sniff out a fake.

God called YOU to lead middle schoolers, not a more polished version of you, or a cooler version, or someone with better stories. God can use the real YOU in the life of a middle schooler. Even if the real you is reserved and awkward, you can still show up in a way that engages students when you are comfortable being who you already are.

So . . .

Show up with **energy**.

Middle schoolers will never be more excited about the material than you are. They will match your energy. If you have a lot of it, they will too. If the vibe you give off is that you just woke up or that you really don't care, they aren't going to care either. If you sound passionate and are excited about what you are teaching, they will also be excited about it. This doesn't mean you have to scream as if you are at a surprise birthday party the whole time. It means you can use passionate language like, "Isn't this so cool?" Or, "This is my favorite part. I am so excited to tell you about this!" Or, "This is so interesting, right?"

Show up **confident**.

Don't let insecurity show up for you. Show up as someone called and prepared to be there because you are. If you look scared to death, they are going to be scared to death for you (or they may take over your talk because they know they can). Don't be scared of them or scared to teach them. Show them you own the room and that you're confident in the message you want to share with them! Don't try and prove you belong—let your confidence come out naturally.

Show up **comfortable**.

Don't show up reviewing your notes or nervously going through slides. Prepare enough to show up and be comfortable. Your students will reflect what you project. You get more comfortable teaching a topic by researching around 90 percent more about a topic than you would ever share in your short lesson. Get to know the information so well that it shows in how you talk about it.

Maybe you are uncomfortable talking about the topic because of the nature of the topic—like the sex series. Then you have to work hard at getting comfortable with it, because they need you to. If you feel awkward teaching a certain topic, they are going to feel awkward about you teaching it. So, talk about it with people you know. Practice it. Say the words and phrases that make you uncomfortable until it gets easier. If you laugh, they'll laugh (and this is okay!). Be so comfortable that you make up for the awkward, natural discomfort that already exists in middle school.

Show up **dressed like you**.

I understand the desire and pressure of wanting to dress "cool" so middle schoolers relate to you more. It makes sense. If we look "old" or "out of style," we fear middle schoolers may write us off or make fun of us. There is some truth in that. However, in my opinion and experience, if middle schoolers know who you are, and you show up confidently and comfortable in who you are, and you talk to middle schoolers like you take them seriously and think they are awesome, they actually don't really care how you dress. However you show up, show up dressed like YOU.

Show up **acting like you**.

God wired you in a specific way on purpose. You don't have to try to communicate in the exact same way someone else communicates. Middle schoolers can tell faster than anyone else when you're trying to be someone you're not. Let your personality show in the way you communicate. Middle schoolers need to see . . .

> people who are outgoing,
> people who are shy,
> people who are loud,
> people who are quiet,
> people who are funny,
> people who are passionate,
> people who are serious.

They need to see all of these facets of different personalities so they can see those exact facets of themselves. This will show them that it's okay to be themselves, that they don't have to act a certain way, and that they just need to be the best version of themselves.

> *"I am a middle-aged mom. I own it. I tell them I have cookies for when they need comfort food, Band-Aids on standby, and mom hugs. I know I am old enough to be their mom, but I am not THEIR mom, so they can talk to me about anything. It really resonates."* —Gina Abbas

The most important thing you can do to fully show up with your own personality is to **understand your speaking voice.**

I had been speaking for a long time before I learned about this, thanks to one of the best communicators on the planet, Jeff Henderson, who I've already mentioned is my friend, pastor, and mentor. Several years ago, he invited me into a three-month coaching cohort of female communicators, wanting to help each one of us grow in our natural gifting. I am forever grateful for his investment in me as a communicator in the church.

As I mentioned earlier, we all prefer to learn in certain ways, but Jeff taught us that we likely speak, teach, or preach in a dominant way as well. He taught us that it's important to understand your speaking voice, because it will allow you to leverage the strength of it and supplement the weakness.

The four speaking voices are the Teacher, the Motivator, the Storyteller, and the Visionary.[54]

Voice	Strength	Weakness
Teacher	Great content; a lot of content	Lack connection
Motivator	Connects easily with the room	Lean more on inspiration than content/clarity
Storyteller	Easily draw people in with great story	Lack direction and purpose of the story
Visionary	Help us see something that does not currently exist	Doesn't clearly articulate how

This was such a breath of fresh air to talk about with the other nine women in the group because it relieved the pressure from having to speak or teach like anyone else. We could just be us—fully us.

I discovered I have a Motivator speaking voice. I love spending time thinking about how to start a talk, or how to make it more fun, and how to get the room interested. That's so much fun for me. Understanding my own speaking voice has helped me lean into how I am naturally wired to communicate, and it has also helped me understand where I need to focus in order to supplement the areas where I am weaker.

The part that requires more focus for me is developing the content—the middle portion of my talk. I always start with Scripture when I begin building the pieces of my talk. As the hardest part of the message to develop, that's what needs to get the most time in my preparation. Like we said in Chapter 3, there are tons of different ways to prepare a talk. There is no right way to do it! Learning your speaking voice can help you leverage your strengths,

"

Be you! You're going to feel a lot of pressure to communicate like someone else, especially when you're first starting out. You don't have to be like anyone else to be a good communicator. You have to find a style (for both delivery and preparation) that works for you and then simply be you when you're speaking. Students (and adults, really) want to be able to connect with a real person—who you really are—and not with who you feel pressure to be. As you get more and more comfortable being yourself while speaking and preparing a talk, your audience will be increasingly able to connect with you and ultimately to hear what it is you want to communicate to them."

—Brett Eddy

JOB	LOCATION	EXPERIENCE
Pastor of Student Ministries at Port City Community Church	Wilmington, NC, USA	20+ years of experience communicating to middle schoolers

Learn more about how Brett prepares to communicate on page 240
Learn more about how Brett prepares to communicate on page 240

bolster your weaknesses, and tailor your speaking voice to the particular environment you're speaking in.

Every time you teach a middle schooler, **show up:** with energy, confident, comfortable, dressed like you, and acting like you.

Reflect & Contextualize

A review of how we need to **SHOW UP:**

    Show up with energy.

    Show up confident.

    Show up comfortable.

    Show up dressed like you.

    Show up acting like you.

What's the most difficult part of showing up for you?

_____

_____

_____

_____

_____

_____

What's the easiest part of showing up for you?

_____

_____

_____

_____

_____

_____

Pause.

Pull out your computer or phone and head to jeffhenderson.com.

Take a few minutes to complete the assessment called Four Voices Assessment.

What is your speaking voice?

_____

_____

What are the strengths and weaknesses of that speaking voice?

Strengths

_____

_____

Weaknesses

_____

_____

What is one thing you need to do to prepare to fully show up next time you speak?

_____

_____

_____

_____

OWN THE ROOM

Have you ever been in front of a room full of middle schoolers and wanted to throw something at them? Have you ever felt like they make it simply impossible for you to teach?

If you have, then you're not alone, because there's something about being in a room full of middle schoolers that leaves you wondering, "Are they even capable of listening?"

The truth is a room full of middle school students requires a lot more room management. Even managing a handful of middle schoolers can feel overwhelming! While you can let middle schoolers in a small group setting have a little more freedom, middle schoolers in a large group space need a lot more structure in order to avoid total and complete chaos. Managing a room full of middle schoolers can be exhausting, frustrating, and even a little bit exhilarating at times.

Honestly, **managing a roomful of young teenagers is an art**. However, when you learn to do it well, you're opening the door to communicating the truth of Scripture more clearly and more loudly than before, cultivating an environment where teenagers want to listen.

There are tons of ways you can become a more dynamic speaker, but here are a few that I've found helpful when it comes to engaging (or re-engaging) middle schoolers:

CHANGE YOUR VOLUME

A great communicator uses their voice to signal middle schoolers when to lean in and listen, and to signal when it's okay to lean back and relax. So, vary your volume. When you are telling a narrative from Scripture, or a story from your life, there should be moments when your volume increases and decreases. You don't want to overdo it or you will exhaust the people listening to you. If you change your volume too often, everything sounds important or equally exciting. But if you underuse this technique, and speak monotone, you would be incredibly boring. So be selective when you vary the volume of your voice. Do this when you want to cue them you are about to make a really important point. When you change the way you speak, students take notice.

CHANGE YOUR PACE

Change the pace at which you're talking. This is especially useful in story-telling. If you are telling a story about a funny or wild moment, the pace at which you are speaking should increase to help build the anticipation. As soon as the pivotal part of the story arrives, you slow your speech down just enough to help middle schoolers feel the tension about to resolve. When you talk quickly, it communicates energy and excitement. When you slow down, it communicates seriousness.

You can also change your pace when building tension. You might get really excited and start talking as fast as you can, but then all of a sudden, you stop. Not because you're glaring at kids who are talking, but because you're making a conscious choice to leave students on the edge of their seats while building this tension. Communicators call that a "pregnant pause," and trust me, it works. All of a sudden, the kids who weren't listening realize you've stopped talking. Just like that, their attention is back on the stage because they're wondering what just happened as you changed your pacing to re-engage them.

CHANGE YOUR BODY LANGUAGE

Your facial expressions, gestures, eye contact, and the way you use your hands and body while speaking have the potential to say a lot more than the words you are actually speaking. According to research, up to 55 percent of communication in a face-to-face environment is non-verbal.[55] That means that body language really matters, and it's especially important that your body language matches what you are trying to communicate with your words too. For example, when you are asking a question, you might use your hands and arms to physically communicate the feeling of "I don't know," while making a face that also looks confused. That makes the question all the more powerful.

When you get to the meat of your talk, and you want students to know you understand them and love them, that's a great place to make eye contact

"

As you continue to learn and read, let me encourage you with this: As a young communicator, I was in a preaching class at seminary. My older brother, who had been preaching for decades, said, 'Heather, be a good student and learn from your profs . . . but just know that you will find your own style and way.' That was gold for me in my journey! You are you. God made you unique and different. Be you. Be smart and learn from others, but be you. Middle schoolers will love you for it!"

—Heather Flies

JOB	LOCATION	EXPERIENCE
Junior High Pastor at Wooddale Church	Minneapolis, MN, USA	29+ years of experience communicating to middle schoolers

Learn more about how Heather prepares to communicate on page 225

with every kid in the room. Imagine making a really personal and vulnerable statement, but you're looking at the back of the room, and not personally connecting with the students in front of you. Your lack of eye contact could cause every middle schooler in the room to miss what you actually said.

Then, there is always the mistake of smiling as you are sharing something serious, like a narrative from Scripture about someone killing someone else. Your smiles are confusing in the context of what you are saying. That's not something to smile about. The opposite is true too. If you don't smile or laugh when something is funny, you look like a serial killer (and middle schoolers will miss the humor).

CHANGE YOUR MOVEMENT

Rather than standing in one place, moving around while you teach can actually work in your favor, especially when you're speaking to a room that has those two (or eight or twenty) distracting students in the audience. Moving toward a certain direction of the stage or room, or walking directly at the student who is talking, while continuing to teach can be an easy and effective way to minimize talking from people in the audience and re-engage those distracted students. This can also help eliminate the need to say things like, "Please stop talking," "Listen up," or "Would you please SHUT UP?!" (Pro tip: I don't recommend using that last one from the stage. "Shut up" is a great example of a borderline word.)

Recently, I was observing a young man named Simon teaching in a middle school ministry. The sixth-grade boys were literally sitting on top of each other on the front right center of the stage. They were touching each other and talking to each other the entire time he was speaking (I am confident this has happened to every person reading this book). Rather than addressing them, hushing them, or asking them to stop, he brilliantly walked right over in front of where they were and continued his lesson three inches from them. It automatically reset their attention and piqued their interest, and they got quiet. Standing ovation, Simon!

Great communicators are comfortable moving around the room as they speak to eliminate their need to use words to redirect attention or behavior.

CHANGE YOUR TONE

Talk with them, not at them. Middle schoolers live in this tension between still being a kid who is unable to make their own decisions about their life (like their schedule, money, or living situations) and having a deep desire for the freedom to make their own decisions (how they spend their money, which parent they spend the weekend with, how late they can stay up, which app they are allowed to download). Talking to them in a way that is not condescending, or parental, or authoritative will help you build trust with them.

The truth is they want to be taken seriously.
They are tired of being talked down to.
They want to be valued.

As the communicator in front of them, we have the opportunity to help them feel like they are taken seriously, that they are important, and that they are valued right now as middle schoolers, even if every adult might not see them that way.

In order to communicate value to a middle schooler, I've noticed really great communicators keep a few things in mind:

1. **Be careful of using condescending language.** This might look like asking demeaning questions or making statements that could make a middle schooler feel "less than" because of the fact they are in middle school. For example, instead of saying, "You're still trying to figure this out," you could say, "We are all on this journey together." This doesn't isolate middle schoolers and instead empowers them to know that it's okay to not have everything figured out yet. It also helps you become more relatable, as an adult acknowledging that you're still figuring it out too.

2. **Be careful of setting too many rules.** The fewer rules you have, the more rules they will follow. Remember, **more rules and more severe consequences do not equate to better behavior.** In fact, it does the opposite! An environment that's rule-heavy creates an atmosphere of rebellion. Middle schoolers want freedom. As hard as it might be sometimes, try to give them a little more freedom than you're comfort-

able with. When you do, they might just give you more attention than they're comfortable with.

3. **Be careful with asking rhetorical questions.** Not because they aren't helpful, but because they may actually answer them and miss that you are just posing a question and not wanting an answer. In fact, if I plan to ask a rhetorical question, I often find myself first saying, "Okay, I am going to ask you something, but I don't want you to actually answer it. I just want you to think about it."

4. **Be careful with how you talk to middle schoolers.** Don't talk down to them. They won't respond to that. If they feel like you understand them and are for them and with them, they will follow you anywhere. Middle schoolers have a deep desire for us to take them seriously. In fact, they not only desire it, but they gravitate toward it. I remember hearing Duffy Robbins say it this way: "Middle schoolers are drawn to the oldest person in the room who takes them seriously." And a great way to take them seriously is to ask them to teach you something.

CHANGE YOUR SET-UP

As a public school teacher, we were encouraged to change the set-up of our classrooms and put different posters, visuals, etc. on the walls every quarter. Why? When you change up a physical environment, you are helping to reset the brain. Plus, looking at the same thing or sitting in the same seat each week for months can feel boring after a while.

Maybe your students typically sit in chairs during the large group message, so changing it up could look like having them sit on the floor with their small groups.

Or maybe you don't typically include a set design or backdrop on stage (or in the front of the room) when you teach. Mix it up by adding some string lights or the series graphic printed on a large poster board.

Try having them sit with their small groups during large group.

Whatever it is, changing your set-up and physical space helps re-engage your students in a way that boosts and improves learning.

"My favorite middle school environment placed a stage in all four corners of the room. The speaker would start on one of them and then throw it to a prop or interactive on the second stage. Prayer happened on the third stage. The kids had to change directions every four to seven minutes. This isn't always possible in large environments, but it was great in a small room of 70 kids." —Crystal Chiang

CHANGE YOUR PRE-SERVICE PRESENCE

As time winds down before it's your turn to speak, rather than hiding in the bathroom practicing your talk, work the room by engaging with the middle schoolers. This will not only calm your nerves, but it will give you a chance to crowdsource your content if needed. If you show your face (and excitement to see them) before you speak, they will be more likely to listen to you because they have already been reminded that you like them.

Speaking to middle schoolers at a camp or weekend retreat? Engaging with students the whole week or weekend that you're with them can be a game-changer in how they are able to connect with you, and you with them. Especially if this is the first time you're meeting that group of students. Being able to use real-time examples and shout-outs of students you've met during the event will help them establish trust in you, and will communicate that you like them. When they know that you like them, they like you too. It all starts with being present throughout the event!

I know that owning a room of middle schoolers is not an easy thing to do. It takes a lot of trial and error. It means trying things that are outside of your natural comfort zone to figure out what works for you. It requires an incredible amount of patience. Like I said before, managing a room full of middle schoolers is an art. When you figure out how to do it well, you'll be able to clearly and confidently communicate truth in an environment where your middle schoolers will want to lean in and listen.

Every time you teach middle schoolers, **own the room**.

Reflect & Contextualize

Describe a time or experience when you felt like you had control of the room.

_____

_____

_____

_____

_____

_____

_____

_____

Describe a time or experience when you felt like you did NOT have control of the room.

_____

_____

_____

_____

_____

_____

_____

_____

Reflect & Contextualize

What aspect of owning the room would you like to work on the next time you communicate to middle schoolers?

Change your volume.
Change your pace.
Change your body language.
Change your movement.
Change your tone.
Change your set-up.
Change your pre-service presence.

Who have you observed who has done this well when communicating to middle schoolers? Describe what they did well.

_____

_____

_____

_____

_____

_____

_____

_____

_____

_____

_____

EXPECT THE UNEXPECTED

At 22 years old, I had just started my first year of teaching middle school health in the public school system just outside of Baltimore, Maryland. About eight weeks into the school year, it was time to teach the "Family Life Unit," also known as the sex education unit. My first two class periods of the day were with eighth-graders.

It was my very first time teaching this unit without another teacher in the room. Everything was going well until we were labeling the male anatomy on a black and white overhead projector—because showing anything else was "too graphic."

An eighth-grade boy, Bryson, must have been a little lightheaded or queasy from labeling his own body part, so he decided to stand up in the middle of class. When he did, he immediately passed out, fell down, and slammed his head into the metal door frame, cracking the back of his head. He hit his head so hard that he went into a seizure.

So, just to paint the picture: Bryson has passed out, blood is everywhere, and now he is foaming at the mouth, making animal noises as he's seizing. The entire class is staring at me as if I am supposed to know what to do! All I could think was, "Where is my mom?" and "Who put me in charge of this classroom?!?"

It's safe to say, I wasn't ready for this. It caught me so off-guard that as soon as the class left, I bawled my eyes out for two hours straight. I couldn't even teach my next class. The principal sat with me as I sniffled and tried to gain control, not only talking me through what to do when a student has a seizure but also what to do when unexpected things happen when you are teaching. Needless to say, they started keeping a wheelchair in my class-room on a daily basis, because this was just the first of many times middle schoolers would pass out in my class while I was teaching. Maybe I am a graphic storyteller or something? A gift and a curse, I suppose.

The longer I have worked with middle schoolers, I have learned that I am not alone when it comes to unexpected things happening while teaching. In fact, I asked my friends on Instagram to share some of the weirdest, most distracting things middle schoolers had done while they were teaching. Here are some examples of what they shared:

A middle schooler . . .

⇨ got up to go to the bathroom, walked into the restroom in the back of the room, and yelled loudly for everyone to hear, "Scream 'HEY, HEY' if you are pooping!"

⇨ farted and then asked, "What are you going to do about it?"

⇨ tied their shoelaces to the chair and face-planted while trying to get up.

⇨ pierced his eyebrow with a safety pin.

⇨ lost a tooth on the front row and tried really hard to hide it, but there was blood everywhere.

⇨ kept their hand raised for a solid eight minutes straight as I tried to finish the lesson.

⇨ blew a bubble and accidentally spit their gum at me.

⇨ put chafing cream on his armpits mid-talk.

⇨ pretended to be a snake and was slithering in between people's legs and under chairs.

⇨ crawled under the stage.

⇨ shot their empty soda can toward the trash can 20 feet away. Missed it, got up, picked up the can, and tried again.

⇨ carried a stuffed cat with her every time she came to group and would pet it during the entire talk.

⇨ literally read a book the entire time I was teaching.

⇨ kept writing down hash marks on a blank piece of paper. NO idea what they were counting.

⇨ stood up during an emotional closing of my talk and started singing "Happy Birthday" to me. It definitely was not my birthday.

⇨ stuck all of his hand in his mouth except for his thumb and just left it there while I taught. There was drool everywhere.

⇨ took a full-blown phone call while sitting in the very front row while the rest of the room was silent and listening to me teach.

I don't have to tell you that middle schoolers are unpredictable. That's what makes them so fun. But when you are teaching and things like this happen, it can be super-distracting. It can also cause you to completely lose your train of thought, or even say something you hadn't planned to say out of reaction that you later regret.

While speaking to middle schoolers on a Sunday morning recently, a boy on the front row started climbing onto the stage. He would move up one step at a time until he was sitting on the stage right next to my feet, facing the crowd. The thing is, he wasn't trying to be funny or distracting. He was quiet, and his face was calm and serious. He just wanted to sit closer, I guess? It was so challenging not to lose my train of thought. I kept wondering if his small group leader or a staff member would step in and call him down from off the stage, but it didn't happen. So, instead of reacting or addressing it from the stage (which would have been an even bigger distraction), and because he was quiet and still listening, I kept teaching with him sitting right there next to me. I have no idea if that was the right thing to do, but it worked (at least that time).

Sometimes the distractions won't be as calm or quiet. One of the biggest frustrations I hear when talking to youth workers is that, oftentimes, students will never stop talking to each other while they're teaching (hello, middle school ministry). It's really a challenge to not let it distract or frustrate you as the communicator. One of the best moves I have seen communicators make in this situation is to continue talking as if the room is silent and listening, and to continue teaching confidently, not letting the talkers take the microphone. In these situations, changing the volume, pace, or tone of your voice, or changing your physical presence in the room, can immediately recapture the talker's attention without you having to address them directly.

Three of the most helpful things you can do when the unexpected happens are:

1. **Use your leaders.** Have your adult leaders sit with their students in the audience. Most often, volunteer leaders choose to sit in the back of the room, but it's more beneficial to you as the communicator to have them dispersed throughout the room to address any behavioral issues they see. That saves you the trouble of trying to do so from stage. However, don't just have them sit with the students. Train them

on what you want them to do when they are sitting with their students and something unexpected happens. Many times, I have had leaders sitting with their students but have no idea what to do, so they do nothing. They might give a verbal reminder, motion for the student to come sit right next to them for the rest of the talk, or pull them aside if the behavior continues. If you're a guest speaker, ask the ministry leader how he or she uses volunteers for crowd control and how you might cue them if things get out of hand.

2. **Have a reaction ready to go.** If something distracting is happening in the room, sometimes it helps to redirect by turning what you're saying into a question for them to discuss with the person next to them. Or, if there is an inside joke that has been happening in the ministry, bring it up. Depending on the situation, you may speak louder, speak faster, speak softer, or stop speaking altogether for a moment. Sometimes, it's helpful to walk over to where the distraction is, while continuing to talk. And sometimes, I've discovered it's best if you just pause and laugh with everyone in the room.

3. **Listen to your natural reaction (sometimes)**. If your natural reaction is appropriate, sometimes that's the best way to acknowledge the distraction and move on from it together as a group. Sometimes, depending on what the distraction is, you literally just need to pause and laugh with everyone in the room. But we are human, so sometimes our natural reaction is to get annoyed and let everyone know it. In my experience, it is never helpful to sound angry or annoyed on stage, even if you feel that way.

Here's another way I think about it: If you have ever been to a rodeo, you know that the bull riding competition is intense to watch. I don't think I breathe the whole time. The cowboy (or cowgirl) either gets thrown off the bull right away, or they stay on for eight seconds and win (and then they get thrown off). In order for them to stay on for eight seconds, they need to follow the movement of the bull. It's like a dance. If they fight the movement, they are thrown off. The same is true for communicating to a middle schooler. Allow for middle schoolers to move (and distract) suddenly and awkwardly, and be ready to move with them. This is how you don't lose them.

"

As someone who did not grow up seeing someone like me on the stage, it is truly a gift for a young person to identify with and hear the Gospel from someone who looks like them, thinks like them, and understands them. When students learn from a diverse group of communicators, they hear the Gospel and see the Kingdom in its fullness. Each communicator has a different teaching style and life experience which allows them to connect with different students in different stages of life, faith, and maturity. Don't just think about diversity in terms of ethnicity, but also gender, age, family life, hobbies, and life experience."

—Katie Matsumoto Moore

JOB

Community Pastor,
Our City Church

LOCATION

Corona, CA,
USA

EXPERIENCE

10+ years of experience
communicating to
middle schoolers

Distractions and disruptions are part of the deal when communicating to middle schoolers, but when they happen, they don't have to rule your talk. Sure, your middle schoolers will throw things across the room, not be able to keep their hands to themselves, or answer everything you ask or wonder out loud. They might even take it to the next level and do something like pull a pickle out of their sock right in front of you and eat it while listening to your talk. Here's the thing: Those disruptions can either throw you off, or you can roll with it, redirect, and continue delivering your message in a way that brings them with you through it.

Every time you teach a middle schooler, **expect the unexpected.**

Reflect & Contextualize

Describe anything unexpected that happened when you or someone else was speaking:

How did the speaker (or you) handle it well?

_____

_____

_____

_____

_____

_____

_____

What is something they (or you) could have tried differently?

_____

_____

_____

_____

_____

_____

_____

_____

If something unexpected happens:

What are you going to do?

_____

_____

_____

_____

_____

_____

_____

_____

What are you going to say?

_____

_____

_____

_____

_____

_____

_____

_____

_____

5. BUILD YOUR TEAMS

TEACHING TEAM

WHY HAVE A TEACHING TEAM?

Maybe you're a volunteer who is already part of a teaching team at your church. If you are, high-five your leader! Maybe you are a Young Life or Fellowship of Christian Athletes leader, and the idea of having a team approach to content sounds glorious. Maybe you're a teacher in a public school who wishes having a team was an option. Believe me, I get that. If you are in a situation where you cannot build a teaching team, jump to page 193. However, if you are someone with the ability to build a team, or if you are part of a teaching team, I think it can be a really helpful way to make sure you are reaching every kid you have been entrusted with, and to steward the gifts your volunteers have been given well.

Here's why . . .

Having a teaching team allows you to multiply yourself. Maybe your ministry is big enough to separate your middle school and high school students, but you are responsible for both environments. It's difficult to prepare and teach two different lessons live. The great thing about having a teaching team is that you can have someone teaching to one group, and you can teach the other. This not only allows you to prepare for one talk, but allows each of you to prepare your talks in a way that best reaches your students where they are developmentally. What your middle schoolers need to hear and how they need to hear it is entirely different from what and how your high schoolers need to hear it.

Having a teaching team allows you to do the most important thing. When you are not the only one able to communicate the large group message to your students, it allows you more time to do the most important thing in your ministry: connect with your leaders and your students. You can act as a small group leader for your volunteers or students rather than split your time between communicator and leader. When you're the communicator, students may feel uncomfortable answering questions about the lesson because they won't want to offend you. If someone else is teaching the lesson, they may be more likely to speak freely about questions, doubts, or areas where they disagree.

Having a teaching team allows you to invite diversity. I believe that every kid needs to see both someone on stage who looks like them and someone on stage who doesn't. T.D. Jakes says it best: "If I don't see me, it's not for me." And, "If I only see me, then I will never understand how big God really is." By building a teaching team, you have the opportunity to make that possible. You can intentionally bring diversity to your stage by presenting your students with communicators of different races, ages, ethnicities, physical abilities, socioeconomic backgrounds, and genders.

Having a teaching team allows your students to hear from different perspectives. Even the best communicators can only speak from lived experience, which means maybe a quarter of the room can relate to your lived experiences. So, when teaching a series on friendship or family, it's important to have a variety of voices from a variety of lived experiences shared in order to relate to each student present in the room.

The truth is that having a teaching team allows you, as the ministry leader, to do what only you can do, and allows you to do even more than that. It can be easy to believe that you have to be the one to teach every single week. Maybe that's not just an expectation you have of yourself, but it's an expectation that others have for you. Doug Fields, one of the best communicators of all time, says it best in his book *Speaking to Teenagers*:

> *"My biggest hurdle during my early years of youth ministry was the twisted thinking that I needed to be the one to teach every week. I thought that since I was the youth pastor, all the teaching was expected from me because of my job title. In addition to that self-imposed expectation, I also carried the unrealistic expectation that I needed to hit a 'home run' with every message. Unfortunately, it took me too many years to learn that both of these expectations were totally unrealistic.*
>
> *I've since figured out that I can't hit a home run every week. Neither can you. And the expectation of teaching every week . . . well, everyone hopes for and expects good teaching, but I've discovered that the good teaching doesn't need to come from me every week.*
>
> *The main issue is that teenagers get good, solid, biblical teaching—whether it comes from me or someone else. I needed to adjust my expectations, deal with my own pride and insecurity issues, rethink how I was managing my time, and encourage other volunteers to help with teaching."*[56]

PICKING YOUR TEACHING TEAM

YAY! Let's build your team!!!!

Building a teaching team is one of my favorite things to do. I love coaching communicators as much as I love communicating. You probably do too!

Below is a list of questions to ask yourself to find out who in your circle may be some of the strongest candidates for your middle school teaching team.

Consider answering each question, and then look for the names that keep recurring!

⇨ Who are the most consistent volunteers?
⇨ Who are the best small group leaders?

⇨ Who is new-ish in their faith?

⇨ Who is the youngest volunteer?

⇨ Who is the oldest volunteer?

⇨ Which volunteer is the best storyteller?

⇨ Which volunteer is the funniest?

⇨ Who is the parent of a middle schooler?

⇨ Who is the life of the party?

⇨ Who is the introvert who everyone loves?

⇨ Who is a worship leader or service host who is great in front of people?

⇨ Who is the person who could hold a mic in front of the room and say nothing, and your middle schoolers would start cheering for them?

⇨ Who are the educators in your church? (Go after the teachers!!!!)

⇨ Who are the college students studying to be teachers?

⇨ Who are your student leaders?

⇨ Who are the high school students who are great role models?

⇨ Who are your middle school students who are interested in talking about their faith with their peers?

⇨ Who is the heartthrob?

⇨ Who is the party starter?

⇨ Who is the most energetic (even if they are an introvert)?

⇨ Who is a volunteer that happens to be the only believer in their family?

⇨ Who is a volunteer who was raised in the church?

⇨ Who is someone that grew up in a different part of the country than you are currently in?

⇨ Who is someone who grew up in the same town the church is located?

⇨ Who comes from a traditional family background?

⇨ Who comes from a non-traditional family background?

⇨ Who do your middle schoolers run up to and say hello to when they arrive?

⇨ Who is someone who participates in the
adult services that the students would love
to see visit the middle school ministry?

⇨ Who is phenomenal at communicating digitally?

⇨ Who has voiced interest in speaking?

⇨ Who has a deep passion for middle schoolers?

⇨ Who has a deep passion for theology?

⇨ Who is really great at talking about how they feel?

⇨ Who do the middle schoolers WISH was
part of the middle school ministry?

⇨ Who is the volunteer who tells middle schoolers
how awesome they are all the time?

⇨ Who would be the best person to speak to the girls?

⇨ Who would be the best person to speak to the guys?

Obviously, there are other things to consider like personal integrity, trustwor-thiness, and if their social media presence says the opposite of what they would be teaching. Keep in mind that we are all on a journey, and nobody is perfect. Sometimes, all somebody needs is a hard conversation, and an opportunity to do something significant (like teach middle schoolers!). Once you've done the character assessment, it's time to train them!!!!

TRAINING YOUR TEACHING TEAM

Now that you have a list of names you want on your team, it's time to train them!

1. **Observe other communicators.**

   When it was time for my semester of student teaching to begin, the best gift my supervising teacher gave me was to go observe other communicators. I didn't only observe great communicators who spoke to adults or high schoolers, but I observed those who teach middle schoolers. I was encouraged to take note of how they man-aged the room, what I noticed about their teaching method and their delivery, and any questions I had for them afterward. I kept track of things that worked great for them but may not work for my personal-ity, as well as things I wanted to try next time I taught. I was required to observe ten different middle school teachers prior to ever teaching my first lesson. I was advised to find at least one thing I would—or would not—do from each teacher.

So, go on a field trip to observe some local middle school teachers or middle school youth pastors. Tune in to a live stream of a middle school service or three. Do it individually or in a group. Then, talk about it!

Our middle school curriculum at Orange provides teaching videos not just for use in the service but to be used as training tools for your developing communicators. Having your communicators watch someone else teach the message will not only help them as they prepare to deliver a message themselves, but it will also help them better understand how to communicate a message to this specific age group. Plus, some people are better visual learners than auditory learners. Showing them a video will go a long way in teaching them how to communicate.

Maybe you just built a team of communicators, which I am guessing all have different strengths. Encourage them to learn from each other! If you have a really great storyteller on your team, ask them to talk about how they prepare a story. They will gain experience by helping another communicator prepare to deliver their story and sermon as well!

2. **Build confidence.**
   You selected each of the people on your teaching team for a reason. Tell them that reason. Cast vision for the diverse teaching team you intend to build, and why representation matters. Tell them you need their perspective, their personality, and their presence. Tell them you need them to be themselves; you don't need them to be a clone of you or any other communicator. When they begin to really believe that you believe in them, they will begin believing in themselves too.

3. **Resource them.**
   Get on the same page. Depending on the makeup of your team, you may have people who have taught in other settings, or people who have never used a microphone. The important thing about building

a team is getting everyone on the same page, equipping them to understand who they are communicating to, and outlining the best practices for communicating to middle schoolers.

Contextualize. If you are teaching from a curriculum, you will need to teach them the skill of contextualizing. This means taking something that is written and making it work for your specific audience.

Are the examples relevant to this group?
Is this the exact tension your students are feeling in this specific context?
Is there an inside joke or a specific application that works for you?

Give them the skills. If you are asking them to write their own talk, you will need to resource them with the skills on how to write a talk. See Chapter 2 for more on that.

Read this book together. One of the reasons this book was created was for this purpose: to help develop teams of people who master teaching middle schoolers. So, buy this book for your teams, go through it together chapter by chapter, and discuss it, practice it, personalize it.

4. **Practice.**
   Encourage them to practice on their own. Practice the lesson by writing it out, running through it in their head, speaking it out loud, using the voice memo app on their phone to record themselves and listen back. One hack I learned from someone much smarter than me is to stand one inch away from a wall and speak directly into the wall—I know this sounds really strange, but when you do this, you can actually hear what you sound like.

   Encourage them to practice in the physical space they will be teaching. Getting comfortable with the room—the stage, the lights, the screens, and even the microphone—helps communicators get one step closer to not being distracted by the newness of the room and enables them to engage with the students in the space as they speak.

   Encourage them to practice in front of others. Invite the teaching team to come early and hear them practice their message and encourage them. Just keep in mind that, depending on timing, this may not be the time to overwhelm them with things to change. The closer this practice round happens to the actual delivery, the more you should focus on encouraging what's already great to increase their comfort level. If you can plan a practice round a few days in advance where they have time to tweak things, that is when suggested changes can be presented.

> *"I was on a teaching team where every Tuesday the whole team met, and that week's speaker delivered the talk to the teaching team for feedback. It's not ALWAYS possible, but it's a great way to do this."* — Crystal Chiang

5. **Provide opportunities.**
Repetition is key in building confidence and growing as a communicator. None of this happens naturally. Speaking to middle schoolers is like building muscle. You can have the right form and know the correct way to lift, but part of it will always come down to how many repetitions, or how many times, you have to practice.

How might you get more reps in?

— Leading meetings
— Leading a volunteer training
— Leading a volunteer pre-service huddle
— Leading small group conversations
— Leading short devotional times
— Sharing their faith story
— Going live on social media
— Pre-recording something for Reels
— Hosting services
— Teaching a lesson live

Give your teaching team opportunities to build up to these.

6. **Be present.**
I remember the first time my friend, Beza, spoke on the stage in front of middle schoolers. I was leading our pre-service volunteer huddle and was running around doing the million things that need

to happen for a service. Beza pulled me aside and was very frustrated with me because she was freaking out in the kitchen about speaking, and I wasn't there to encourage her, pray with her, and assure her she was going to do great. I realized in that moment that I had forgotten the nerves that come with doing this for the first time. Be with your people as they step out in faith to lead the next generation. They won't always need you this much, but they will the first few times.

7. **Encourage a growth mindset.**
   The first time my friend, Chuck, taught a message in our middle school ministry, he spoke for a total of five minutes. He had planned to speak for 15 minutes, but was so focused on getting the sentences right that he forgot to connect with the students in the room by inviting them into his message. His nerves caused him to rush through the main points of his message, and he abruptly wrapped up saying, "And that's all I've got." It was silent in the room for a moment afterward because the shortest sermon ever abruptly ended. But the best part? Middle schoolers are so forgiving. They loved Chuck. Chuck was the right one to be up there because the middle schoolers started clapping and cheering for Chuck. They loved having a short message so they could go hang out with their small group.

8. **Don't expect perfection.**
   One of the most important things about building a teaching team is giving them feedback on what they did really well, and what they should focus on next time. I find it best to start this conversation with a high-level compliment, and then ask these questions:

   How did you feel about it overall?
   What would you do the same next time?
   What would you do differently?

   After I give them a chance to evaluate themselves, I offer my feedback. I don't necessarily follow the "compliment sandwich" type of feedback, but I do mix positive feedback with ideas of things to try for the next time.

So often, our constructive feedback focuses on how to make it better, but growing communicators need to hear what worked really well so they intentionally continue to do that. If they don't know what and why it worked, they won't be able to repeat it again.

I have also learned that overwhelming growing communicators with five things to do next time typically results in them not wanting to communicate again, or psyching themselves out. I like to give them one goal to focus on for the next time.

After Chuck's abrupt Saturday night message, he had a chance to debrief it with our team, tweak a few things, and get ready to deliver the same message on Sunday. With the first-time nerves out of the way, his second delivery made it to the nine-minute mark. He was getting better with every rep, and we were going to celebrate that. Maybe you are wondering if having a beginner communicator sharing the Good News to middle schoolers and doing a very average job is a good thing. In my opinion, showing middle schoolers an adult who loves them and is willing to step out of their comfort zone to talk about what a relationship with Jesus has done in their life is always a win. Maybe that lesson is even more powerful than the words Chuck spoke!

9. **Rally the team.**

   If you are building a teaching team, it's about more than just having people to schedule to teach each weekend.

   I have been part of teams my entire life.
   Soccer teams.
   Basketball teams.
   Specials teams (this was the team of teachers
   who taught non-core subjects).
   Volunteer teams.

   I love being on a team.

   Being on a team means you have people who you
   show up for, and who show up for you.
   Being on a team means you are all getting better

together, not just getting better alone.
Being on a team means you are all working toward the same goal,
even if the means to reach that goal looks different for each person.
Being on a team means you have a group of people
cheering for you, not competing with you.

When building a teaching team for your middle school ministry, it's
important to build this culture into the team. How? Be it yourself. Talk
about it. Encourage it.

It's much easier to step out in faith together than it is alone.
And it's much easier to leave a role you play than a team you love.

Rally the team.

SCHEDULING YOUR TEACHING TEAM

There were nine of us on the middle school teaching team in the ministry
I led. My goal was to teach less than 50 percent of the time. There was
a season where I only taught 25 percent of the time in order to give my
teaching team opportunities to practice.

Why? A few reasons.

1. Teaching a message isn't the only part of middle school ministry that
    deserves attention from the ministry leader. I had other parts of the
    ministry that mattered just as much—like how connected the small
    group leaders felt, or how we were doing in welcoming first-time
    guests, or building our "host" team of volunteers, or pouring into our
    student-led worship team.

2. Instead of putting my energy into preparing my own lesson, I needed
    to put my energy into cheering on other communicators who could
    communicate from a different perspective.

3. If I choose to leave or if God calls me away from this post, building a
    teaching team ensures there is a team of people to bridge the transi-
    tion from one ministry leader to the next.

I realize that may not be possible in your role. I have met many youth pastors who were hired to teach every Sunday as the sole influence on their students. In these situations, you may not be able to hand the honor of teaching off to a volunteer, but is it possible to teach the message and creatively incorporate others into your message somehow?

To read Scripture?
To tell a personal story?
To do an interview or Q&A?
To share an application point?
To pray?

Or maybe building a teaching team in your context is just not an option, at least for now, but you still want to incorporate diversity, introduce new perspectives, and multiply yourself when it comes to the teaching time in your ministry. One way to do that without having to build a team is through showing teaching videos that include a diverse group of communicators and perspectives. Teaching videos can serve as your teaching team for now, as you work toward building your own team in the future.

As you teach middle schoolers, **build your teaching team.** While it allows you to multiply yourself, promotes diversity, and gives your students the opportunity to hear from different perspectives, it also allows you to do what only you can do: invest relationally into your leaders, students, and parents.

Reflect & Contextualize

Who are some communicators that you have learned from personally? What did you learn from them?

_____

_____

_____

_____

_____

_____

What's your plan to have your team . . .

Observe other communicators:

_____

_____

_____

Build their confidence:

_____

_____

_____

Get resourced:

_____

_____

_____

Practice:

_____

_____

_____

Give opportunities:

_____

_____

_____

Experience your presence and support:

_____

_____

_____

Embrace a growth mindset:

_____

_____

_____

Not aim for perfection:

_____

_____

_____

Rally the team:

_____

_____

_____

What percentage of time are you the primary communicator for
your ministry?

_____

What percentage would you like to move toward?

_____

What holds you back from letting others communicate
to your students?

_____

_____

Pause. Pull out your calendar.

Are there any upcoming meetings one of your team members
could lead?

_____

_____

Is there a testimony or interactive that you could give them to lead?

_____

_____

Are any of them ready to teach a full lesson?
When could they teach that?

_____

_____

_____

"

Allowing others to speak into your leadership will not only grow your reach as a leader, but also cultivate a culture of ownership and creativity."

—Kellen Moore

JOB	LOCATION	EXPERIENCE
Next Generation Pastor, Our City Church	Corona, CA, USA	14+ years of experience communicating to middle schoolers

FEEDBACK TEAM

Asking for feedback can be terrifying at times. Especially when you know you didn't do a great job. It can be especially terrifying when you ask the wrong people for feedback.

If you are interested in building a feedback team, I think it's important to identify who you could receive constructive feedback from. And instead of asking for general feedback, ask for specific feedback from that person. That gives them the opportunity to speak into an area where they may be most helpful.

Here is a list of the people on my feedback team and an example of a pointed question I ask them:

Team Member	Question I Ask Them
The person who changed my slides	How did I cue you in transitioning my slides?
The Ministry Leader or Teaching Team lead	What's one thing I can focus on for the next service?
A small group leader I trust	How did your small group conversation go?
A middle school expert	Were there any words, phrases, or concepts that needed to be broken down more?
Someone who knows me really well	Did I seem like myself up there?
A mentor	What should I absolutely do again? What is one thing I can focus on improving for next time?

It's always best if you can ask a number of people for feedback. Just know that everyone may have a different opinion, and you will have to sort through the feedback like you sort your laundry.

At Orange, when we teach students to identify mentors and feedback-givers in their lives, we usually ask them to find people who . . .

⇨ make wise decisions in their own lives.

⇨ love you enough to tell you what you don't want to hear.

Those are the same kinds of people you and I need to give us feedback when we communicate—people who love middle schoolers well in their own role and people who love us enough to tell us the truth, not just hype us up (although hype people are important too!).

I was lucky to have a season of working for middle school ministry legend, Tom Shefchunas, at North Point Ministries. I looked up to "Shef" for his strategic mind, and valued his knowledge of the middle school mind, middle school content, and high standards for communicating. There were numerous times Shef would come watch me speak and give me feedback.

Sometimes it was just a suggestion of one word to change: "Don't say book, because it was actually a letter."

Sometimes he would have a question for me: "Did you make eye contact with the kid who would not stop talking on purpose?"

Sometimes he offered mainly compliments and confidence building: "Watching you teach is reminding me of things I used to do as an educator that I have forgotten," or "You are motivating me to start my talks with more energy."

Sometimes he would ask if I spent enough time preparing and if I had lost my train of thought at a certain point in my message.

Sometimes he would tell me to shave off parts of my story that were not relevant and kind of distracting.

Sometimes he would tell me things like, "Don't smile when you are talking about how David had Uriah killed in battle to cover up his affair with Bathsheba. You are talking about murder, not puppies."

Sometimes he would say I took too long on the front end to get to the truth section, and to jump in quicker.

Sometimes he would tell me to stop pacing while I talked.

Sometimes the feedback would come between services so I could make immediate changes, and sometimes I didn't get feedback.

Sometimes he scheduled a debrief meeting with me the following week to talk through things, pick my brain and methods, and draw things on his white board.

Shef was my boss and the leader of the teaching team, so his feedback was expected. But one thing was evident: Shef was committed to helping me become the best dang communicator I could become, and I am forever grateful for that.

We can be this kind of leader and feedback giver for our teaching team!

As scary as it might feel, if you ever have the opportunity to invite someone you look up to as a communicator to hear you speak and provide you with feedback, I encourage you to make the ask.

SELF-EVALUATION

The most effective communicators I know, no matter how long they have been communicating, have the discipline to go back and listen to or watch their talk.

Transparently, this is the hardest part for me.

- ⇨ The sound of my own voice annoys me.
- ⇨ I don't love hearing how hard I am on my "S" sound.
- ⇨ I thought that hat looked so much better than it actually did.
- ⇨ Why am I pacing again?
- ⇨ I totally forgot to break down the second half of that verse.
- ⇨ Am I having a hard time breathing?
- ⇨ I sound like I lost my train of thought there. I never connected my story to the tension I was trying to make.
- ⇨ That was funny, but I could have delivered it differently to get an even bigger laugh.
- ⇨ I bet middle schoolers were counting the number of times I said "like."

Reflect & Contextualize

On a scale of 1 to 10, how often do you ask for feedback?

1 **2** **3** **4** **5** **6** **7** **8** **9** **10**

On a scale of 1 to 10, how comfortable are you with asking for feedback?

1 **2** **3** **4** **5** **6** **7** **8** **9** **10**

Who is currently (maybe unofficially?) on your Feedback Team?

_____

_____

_____

_____

Who do you want on your Feedback Team?

_____

_____

_____

_____

What feedback have you been given that was helpful?

_____

_____

_____

_____

_____

_____

_____

_____

What feedback have you been given that was hard to hear?

_____

_____

_____

_____

_____

_____

_____

_____

_____

If you are anything like me, you are harder on yourself than anyone else could possibly be.

The best part about self-evaluation is that you can say the hard things to yourself, and you have the power to make the changes. We are all unaware of the weird things we do with our mouth, our hands, or filler words we unintentionally say.

The next time you speak to middle schoolers, record yourself. Audio is great, but recording a video is even better. Watch or listen to it back, and then, ask yourself some of these questions to evaluate:

1. What's one thing you did that you definitely want to do next time?
2. What's one thing you did that you definitely don't want to do next time?
3. What went really well?
4. What would you change about your message?
5. What's one thing you wish you would have done differently?

YOU are a part of your own feedback team.

Every time you teach middle schoolers, **build your feedback team.**

Reflect & Contextualize

How do you feel about having a teaching team approach?

_____

_____

_____

_____

_____

_____

_____

_____

What percentage do you want to teach in a given ministry year compared to how much you want to give away?

_____

_____

_____

_____

_____

_____

_____

_____

_____

_____

What qualities are you looking for in someone who might be on your teaching team?

_____

_____

_____

_____

_____

_____

_____

_____

_____

WHO do you want on your teaching team? Why? Jump back to the list of questions on page 177 as a starting place!

_____

_____

_____

_____

_____

_____

_____

_____

_____

_____

Reflect & Contextualize

How hard is it for you to re-watch or listen to yourself teach?

_____

_____

_____

_____

Pause.

Pull up your last talk and watch/listen to it.

Record your observations here:

What's one thing you did that you definitely want to do next time?

_____

_____

_____

_____

What's one thing you did that you definitely don't want to do next time?

_____

_____

_____

_____

_____

What went really well?

_____

_____

_____

_____

_____

_____

What would you change about your message?

_____

_____

_____

_____

_____

What's one thing you wish you would have done differently?

_____

_____

_____

_____

_____

_____

CONCLUSION

HEYOHHHHH!!!!
You made it to the end!
(Well, almost. Don't miss the Bonus Content after this conclusion . . . it's GOLD.)

Maybe at this point you are thinking:

⇨ This was great, but my main takeaway is that I need to spend MORE
time preparing, and I don't have MORE time to give.

⇨ This was an average book. I wish she would have talked about how
to do this in a combined ministry environment (insert brain exploding
emoji here).

I get it. You don't have much more time to dedicate to preparing for
MORE hours. I honestly have never met a youth pastor, teacher, or
volunteer who was not overworked and had extra time on their hands.
There is so much to juggle.

The truth is, communicating to middle schoolers DOES take more time, for
all the reasons we talked about in this book already.

But you can do this.
I promise you can.

There may need to be a season of reworking your schedule or hand-
ing things off in order to have the margin you need. What hangs in the
balance—influencing middle schoolers to develop an everyday faith—is
TOO IMPORTANT.

Take it one step at a time.
YOU GOT THIS.

If you speak in a combined ministry environment, first, let me say, I like
you a lot. You didn't have to pick up a book specific to one age group in
the room, but you did. You are really good at what you do. And you have a
really hard job.

Secondly, I knew you would ask this . . . which is why I included a response to this exact question on page 216 (cue the confetti). Navigating the combined environment is not for the faint of heart.

KEEP GOING!!!

Communicating to middle schoolers requires patience, time, and a lot of grace.

Because middle schoolers can be incredibly exhausting to manage and can be incredibly disruptive when you teach, it's easy to get discouraged as a youth leader. It's easy to want to quit or ask someone else to teach so you don't have to.

But here's the thing:

They need you.
We need you.

We need people who will invest in the art of communicating to middle schoolers. We need people who are going to be okay with failing a lot as they figure out what works best for them, their personality, their context, and their students.

What works for me may not work for you.
What works for the person down the road may not work for you.

But it might.
And it's worth a try.

It's okay to totally bomb a message as you are figuring this out, but it's not okay to stay there.

One of my heroes and favorite coaches of all-time is the legendary Coach John Wooden. He led his UCLA Men's Basketball team to a stunning 10 NCAA Championships in 12 years. A statistic like that makes me want to pay attention to what he paid attention to. Wooden says, "*You will find that success and attention to details, the smallest details, usually go hand in hand.*" He was notorious for insisting on improving the smallest details of everything his players did, down to the way they put on their socks. If you have never read about this, go buy a book called *Wooden: A Lifetime of Observations and Reflections On and Off the Court.*[57]

Coach John Wooden was right. Becoming better at whatever it is you're doing requires attention to the smallest details and making changes that might not seem like that big of a deal in the moment. That's true in basketball, and it's true when it comes to communicating to middle schoolers. I like to say it this way:

Great middle school communicators aren't 100 percent better than every other communicator. They are one percent better in 100 different ways.

All of the things listed in this book are one percent ways to make our delivery better.

We have one shot to help this generation of middle schoolers understand a loving God who wants an everyday relationship with each and every one of them.

The words we use to do this matter.
The way we use them matters.
The way we break down the truths of Scripture matter.
Our analogies matter.
Our illustrations matter.
Our interactives matter.
Our content matters.
Our delivery matters.

So . . .

What's your one percent?

What's one small detail that may make a huge difference in the way you communicate to middle schoolers?

Cheering you on forever!

Ashley

I would love to hear from you!
ashleybohinc.com
ABohinc@thinkorange.com
@ashleymariebohinc

BONUS CONTENT

COMMUNICATING DIGITALLY

I am convinced that people who work with middle schoolers are the most creative, innovative, and strategic people on the planet. I have watched youth workers stop at nothing to get and keep the attention of a sixth or seventh or eighth-grader for years, but nothing has ever tested our flexibility or innovation quite like . . .

March 2020.

You know what I'm talking about. In a matter of weeks, our team watched youth workers around the world go from teaching in live environments to innovating a way to teach online—often with less than 24 hours notice.

It was inspiring.

It was also exhausting.

Not all middle schoolers have social media yet,
many have to share a tablet, phone, or computer
(if they have access to one at all),
some need permission to download certain apps
or participate in digital gatherings,
not every middle schooler has access to Wi-Fi,
and most have rules around where and when
they can use a phone or tablet.

Suddenly, the tension we all already felt about how to reach middle schoolers Monday through Saturday became front and center and more important than ever.

Pretty quickly, we all learned that digital is not the same as "in-person plus a live stream." It was a new environment that required a new strategy, and watching people like YOU develop that strategy has been awe-inspiring.

In the early days of the pandemic, many of us assumed the digital strategy for teaching (in classrooms and in ministry) would be temporary. We thought it would pass as quickly as the pandemic (remember when we thought it'd be over by Spring!?), but what we learned is there are plenty of reasons to maintain a digital teaching strategy even if the world returns to "normal."

You might consider keeping a digital strategy to reach . . .

⇨ student athletes who can't attend services.
⇨ students whose parents are divorced and are only in town every other week.
⇨ students in foster care who aren't always placed near the church.
⇨ students with health needs that prevent them from large gatherings.
⇨ students living in places with school closures due to weather events.
⇨ students who are introverts and open up in a small group but aren't comfortable in a larger group.
⇨ students who are already in an online school and prefer digital community.

In these cases, technology is (virtually) on your side.

The point is, even if the initial reason you started using digital teaching changes, the benefits of offering an online option are obvious. It's too powerful of a platform and too big of an opportunity to NOT think about strategically.

Here are some digital platforms middle school ministry leaders across the world are experimenting with when it comes to communicating with middle schoolers digitally:

⇨ YouTube
⇨ Instagram (Grid, Stories, Reels, LIVE, and whatever else they have added since I wrote this book.)
⇨ Snapchat
⇨ TikTok
⇨ Zoom
⇨ Google Meet
⇨ Discord

⇨ Twitch
⇨ Texting
⇨ FaceTime
⇨ WhatsApp
⇨ Marco Polo
⇨ Telegram

The amazing thing about digital platforms is it's about more than just a one-hour gathering once a week. As my friend and online pastor Dave Adamson writes in his book *MetaChurch: How to Use Digital Ministry to Reach People and Make Disciples*, "Digital platforms create opportunities for church leaders to stay connected with people for the other 167 hours of the week."[58] We can reach students and communicate to students digitally in 15-second video clips if we are leveraging our social media and digital platforms to the best of our ability.

So how do we make the most out of our digital teaching?

After watching some leaders around the country leverage their platforms masterfully, here's what we've learned:

It's NOT just a livestream of the in-person environment. Just like a physical environment, students who show up to a digital environment are all asking the same question, *"Is this for me? Is this designed with people like me in mind? Am I welcome here?"*

A few ways we can let middle schoolers know they are welcome in a digital environment:

1. Have a host just for the digital group.
2. Use your students' names so they feel seen and that they belong.
3. Understand technology, practice it, and make sure it runs smoothly.
4. Don't just push information; invite conversation.
5. Offer content and engagement opportunities on multiple platforms so students who use THAT platform have a place.
6. Tell students you're glad they're here . . . don't just use it as a place to ~~invite~~ guilt them into showing up in person.
7. Invite your middle schoolers to plan or lead portions of the digital experience.

Okay, they feel welcome, and now it's time for the lesson portion of the digital experience.

Here is a list of things I have observed stellar youth leaders do when communicating with middle schoolers digitally:

⇨ Pre-record content and share it on multiple platforms.

⇨ Go LIVE on multiple platforms.

⇨ Include middle schoolers in the planning and execution of digital environments.

⇨ Show behind-the-scenes footage to enhance authenticity.

⇨ Do giveaways and use prizes, mailing out swag, sending candy via Amazon Prime or DoorDashing food faves.

⇨ Consider offering bite-size pieces of information, or some kind of connection piece, during peak times middle schoolers may be using that specific digital platform.

⇨ It is important to consider the digital platforms middle schoolers may be engaging with, but it's also important to consider what the parents feel comfortable with since a majority of middle schoolers need their parent's permission to download certain apps. This is yet another reason why posting on multiple platforms is important.

⇨ Break up the lesson so there isn't a talking head for 18 minutes. Teach for one to three minutes and ask them to respond or discuss.

— By the time you read this, digital platforms may have changed (again). For example, in 2014, the average length of a YouTube video was 4 minutes and 20 seconds. In August 2021, the team at Statista published a report showing that the average length of a video on YouTube had increased to 11 minutes and 42 seconds. If middle schoolers are watching YouTube videos for 11 minutes and 42 seconds, that's great news for us, as communicators.[59] Now, that might seem like a long time to teach digitally, but jump back to page 132 for more on this. Remember, how we use the minutes we teach is what matters most in keeping their interest.

Communicating digitally can be especially challenging because the natural energy that comes from being in a room together is missing. This means great digital communicators show up with more energy and more excitement, so the energy translates through a screen, all while walking the fine line of making sure it doesn't come across as inauthentic or cheesy. Creativity and energy are KEY for communicating digitally! Just like an in-person environment, preparation is crucial.

I have observed some rock star communicators make their digital lesson incredibly engaging, especially since the pandemic began. Here are some ideas I've pulled from them:

⇨ Pause throughout your talk and have students do something.

⇨ After finishing a story about your favorite vacation, pause and ask students to change their virtual background pictures to a place they've always wanted to visit.

⇨ Have them describe their week by posting six emojis in a row on the screen (one emoji for each day).

⇨ Keep the talk active. Just because you are communicating via screen doesn't mean you (or the students) have to be seated still the entire time. Use discretion, but allow yourself and the students to stand or even dance if needed.

⇨ Use props. Props translate very well on screen! You can also encourage students to find their own props wherever they are—students love to feel like you are connected to them in their environment.

⇨ Show appropriate video clips and illustrations that will accompany your talk.

⇨ Use the chat feature!

Here are some practical cues I have seen ministry leaders around the world use to engage middle schoolers in the chat feature during a lesson:

⇨ On a scale of 1-10 . . . drop your number in the chat.

⇨ Drop any red emoji if . . .

⇨ What is one word you would use to describe . . .

⇨ Give a shout out to somebody who . . .

⇨ That was a great example, Jasmine! Everybody show Jasmine some love in the chat . . .

⇨ I am going to show you this YouTube clip, and I want you to drop in the chat anything that surprised you, or any questions this brings up . . .

⇨ Everybody vote in the chat . . .

Don't be afraid of the silence from students keeping themselves on mute. If your students attended school digitally during the pandemic, they were most likely required to keep themselves on mute and have formed this as a habit. They also probably think they are being respectful by staying on mute, and maybe they won't come off mute unless everybody does. You, as the communicator, must figure out ways not to let silence become awkward by not letting it affect you. In other words, plan ahead what you will do or say in the silent moments. A great way to create energy when communicating digitally is playing fun background music. The music fills the silence and helps middle schoolers feel like something is happening.

Also, don't fret if you ask a question that no one comes off of mute to answer. Ask concrete, pointed questions and encourage them to use chat features as an alternative.

It's also likely that middle schoolers may be distracted by things happening in the room wherever they are watching from . . .

pets may walk across their keyboard (so. many. pets.),
baby sister starts crying,
an Amazon package was just delivered,
Granddad walks into the room.

Unfortunately, we can't control when that happens, but we can control how we respond. We can either let it distract us and discourage us, or we can ignore it. Or better yet, we can leverage it for engagement and energy. It all depends on WHEN it happens.

Here are some things we can all do to improve as digital communicators:

⇨ Learn as much as you can about the digital platform you are communicating on. The more you learn about it, the more you will understand how to present your content around the strengths of the platform.

⇨ Watch other people do it and take notes.

⇨ Watch other people on the specific platform you are communicating on to understand how to better leverage it.

⇨ Build a feedback team who understands digital communication.

⇨ If you are pre-recording content, watch other people's pre-recorded content and see what you can pick out.

⇨ Keep doing it and keep trying new things.

⇨ Remember that communicating digitally sometimes feels like starting your reps over again. Don't get discouraged!

Many of the things we talked about in this book thus far translate to communicating digitally, such as object lessons, props, and humor to make things more engaging. We just need to leverage the right communication channels.

If you plan to communicate digitally, either pre-recorded or live,
keep it shorter than in-person,
get to the point quicker than in-person, and
be more energetic than in-person.

Reflect & Contextualize

Take some time and research the 10 most used digital platforms by middle schoolers currently.

Google it. Text a bunch of middle schoolers. Ask the social media world!

On a scale of 1–10, how familiar are you with each of these digital platforms? Drop a number next to each platform.

1. _____

2. _____

3. _____

4. _____

5. _____

6. _____

7. _____

8. _____

9. _____

10. _____

Before you go any further, look up what each of these platforms are and how they are used.

What did you learn?

_____

_____

_____

_____

_____

_____

_____

_____

From your list above, circle the top three digital platforms you know YOUR middle schoolers are currently using.

Dream for a moment: How might you use each of these digital platforms to connect to or communicate truth with middle schoolers?

_____

_____

_____

_____

_____

_____

_____

_____

_____

COMMUNICATING IN A COMBINED MIDDLE AND HIGH SCHOOL ENVIRONMENT

SO . . .

You've read this book, but you are still wondering . . .

⇨ *"How am I supposed to do that when I have a combined group of middle and high school students?"*
⇨ *"How can I make sure to help my middle schoolers win without losing my high schoolers?"*
⇨ *"How can I balance communicating to both middle school and high school well while being the only leader in the room?"*
⇨ *"I actually prefer to keep my middle and high schoolers combined, but I would like to know how to reach my middle schoolers better."*

Excellent questions.

The really direct answer to these questions is that although it IS possible, it IS a challenge to reach both middle and high schoolers WELL in a combined environment.

We know that . . .
We will reach middle schoolers best when there is an environment created specifically for middle schoolers.
We will reach high schoolers best when there is an environment created specifically for high schoolers.

BUT.
We know having unique environments for each is not always possible for a lot of reasons:

budget,
space,
staffing,
volunteers,
or time.

So how do we do it in the best possible way in a combined environment?

First, you need to know that you CAN communicate well in a combined environment. Have you ever watched a family movie with lines only grown-ups understood and enjoyed? While at the same time, the movie powerfully connected with an audience of all ages? It all comes down to lens. Here's what I mean: In our preparation process, we need to be thinking through the middle school AND high school lens. This will be where the teaching team and feedback team we build will be crucial in helping us not to forget either audience.

Preparing to teach in a combined environment will (and should) require even more time. If we aren't strategic and intentional about it, we will automatically lean toward the age group we naturally prefer and forget a lens. Like a well-written movie, it can never be about preparing for one audience, expecting the other audience to listen in. Our message is too important to approach it in this way.

Here are a few takeaways I have observed from ministry leaders who do their best to reach both middle schoolers and high schoolers in a combined environment:

⇨ Be careful not to make jokes with high schoolers at the expense of the middle schoolers in the room.
  — For example, they avoid saying things like: "Remember back when you were 12 inches shorter, and still into wearing cat-ear headbands, with a cat tail attached to your bottom?"

⇨ For every example they give, they give one directly for high schoolers and one directly for middle schoolers.
  — For example, they may say something like: "If you are a middle school student, you may be asking something like _____. If you are a high schooler, this might be a bit different for you. You might be wondering _____."

⇨ When they don't differentiate between the two, they choose examples that both middle and high school students can relate to.
  — Things both age groups may be able to relate to: fights with friends, trying out for a team, embarrassing moments, holiday traditions, family dynamics, vacations.

— Things middle schoolers may not be able to relate to that high schoolers do: driving a car, college visits, taking the SAT, prom or homecoming, dating.

⇨ When unpacking a concept, great communicators make sure to explain what it is, what it means, how it is connected (is it hitting the middle schoolers in the room?) and why it matters (for the high schoolers in the room).[60]

— Middle schoolers may need to talk about factors that create emotion.

— High schoolers may need to analyze how emotions affect behavior.

— Middle schoolers may need to predict others' feelings in a variety of situations.

— High schoolers may need to analyze similarities and differences between one's own and others' perspectives.

— Middle schoolers may need to analyze ways to create positive relationships with others.

— High schoolers may need to evaluate the effects of asking for sup- port from others and providing it.[61]

⇨ They always consider that, developmentally, a high schooler can lean back into where a middle schooler's brain is because they have been there before. It's much more difficult for a middle schooler to speed up brain maturity and think like a high schooler.

— Because of this, they choose to use vocabulary that middle schoolers can grasp but isn't condescending toward high school- ers. They also don't use the vocabulary broken down in a way that talks down to a middle schooler or make it obvious that this is why they are saying something. This isn't a time to say, "Let me say it simpler for the middle schoolers in the room." It's a fine line.

— Jump back to Chapter 1 for some specific examples.

⇨ They empower both high school AND middle school students to be "student leaders" in the ministry. When there is only one age group of student leadership, it indirectly sends a message that this environment is really only for one age demographic.

— They train leaders who are high school students to be the biggest support and champion of the leaders who are middle school students so the rest of the group follows suit.

⇨ They have designated a trusted Middle School Champion and High School Champion to run their talks by on the teaching and feedback teams. These people give feedback about how to be more phase inclusive and flag anything that may be an issue for the phase they champion.

— Some even have more than one!

— Don't forget to lean into the educators in your church. They are trained to do this!

⇨ They are selective in what interactive elements they include in their sermon.

— Showing a video clip or picture works for both audiences.

— The content of the video or picture is where you will experience tension. Great communicators consider some middle schoolers aren't allowed to watch certain shows or movies, so showing a clip from something their parent wouldn't approve of or allow them to watch in entirety may not be the best interactive in a combined environment.

⇨ They have equipped their small group leaders to connect any dots that were not connected, or lead their middle school students through an activity to take something incredibly abstract and make it more concrete.

— Great communicators are humble enough to realize that they can't do from the stage what a small group leader can do in their circles. They figure out ways to hype up the small group leaders throughout their message so students are ready to contextualize the truth for their age group.

— You may also be the small group leader for your students. In these situations, you can STILL hype yourself up and set yourself up for a win later. "If you are wondering what I mean by this, I cannot wait until we break for small group because I have an incredible activity planned for us to break this down." While leading a combined small group, consider asking questions to specific students in your group. For example: "Derek, what is one example of . . .?" "Dom, why do you think . . .?" You can ask the middle school-specific questions to the middle schoolers, and the high school-specific questions to the high schoolers. Basically, you are a magician and the best darn juggler on the planet.

⇨ They have a designated area for their middle schoolers to sit and a designated area for their high schoolers to sit. This way, the middle schoolers aren't pushed to the back of the room or intimidated or blocked by a really tall high schooler from seeing what is happening in the front of the room.
  — I have actually seen this work really well and also not work great. It really all depends on your church culture.

⇨ They may not be able to split their group for weekly programming but choose to split the group for events, or even just once a month!
  — This is a brilliant way to begin experimenting with what works for your specific context.

⇨ They are always working toward an official split. It may be three (or nine) years down the road, but they are always aiming for environments that allow them to turn the volume up on communicating to that specific phase.
  — If you have two middle schoolers and two high schoolers, and no other leaders, the split is likely not going to happen for a while. That's okay! This is where you have a chance to become the best combined environment communicator on the planet by considering what each phase needs. The sheer fact that you read an entire book about how to do this better is evidence that you are WINNING.

— If you are still not convinced they eventually need to be split, and you would prefer to keep the middle schoolers in a high school environment based on the fact that they bring a good energy, I would encourage you to reconsider what a win is for both phases.

— If you want to know more, take a deep dive into the science behind learning and development. A great place to start is to read *It's Just a Phase—So Don't Miss It* by Kristen Ivy and Reggie Joiner.

It's not easy to implement best practices for each phase in a combined environment, but ***it is possible.*** You got this!

Reflect & Contextualize

Do you prefer communicating to middle schoolers or high schoolers? Why?

_____

_____

_____

_____

_____

_____

Who is your Middle School Champion—the person who will always help you look through everything with a middle school lens?

Who is your High School Champion—the person who will always help you look through everything with a high school lens?

How many middle school students do you
have attending on a weekly basis?

Drop the names of five middle schoolers so you picture them when
you are preparing:

1. _____

2. _____

3. _____

4. _____

5. _____

How many high school students do you
have attending on a weekly basis?

Drop the names of five high schoolers so you picture them when
you are preparing:

1. _____

2. _____

3. _____

4. _____

5. _____

*If you are considering splitting your middle schoolers and
high schoolers into their own unique environments, visit
OrangeStudents.com/split-kit for a free guide to walk you through
that decision.*

VARIOUS WAYS TO PREPARE YOUR DELIVERY

I have invited some of my dear friends, who are experts at communicating to middle schoolers, to share what works for them. There is no right or wrong way to prepare, but like we all have a learning style preference, we each have a preferred preparation process as well.

If you are trying to figure out how you best prepare, I want to challenge you to first read through all of these different ways to prepare. Then, try some or all of these ways out. In fact, you might need to try them out multiple times. As you do, you'll quickly learn what works best for you, what absolutely does not work for you, what's helpful, and what's not.

A NOTE FROM

Heather Flies

JOB	LOCATION	EXPERIENCE
Junior High Pastor at Wooddale Church	Minneapolis, MN, USA	29+ years of experience communicating to middle schoolers

Instagram: @heatherflies

I'm just giddy that you are taking the time to read about communicating with middle schoolers! They are my favorite people in the universe! I believe they are capable of so much more than most adults give them credit for, and they deserve our best. I hope you can believe that too!

As I explain my communication process, I feel the need to offer a few disclaimers.

- ⇨ I love to talk. A lot.
- ⇨ I am an extreme extrovert and am energized by a room packed with people.
- ⇨ One of my spiritual gifts is teaching.
- ⇨ In college, I majored in Communication and minored in Writing.
- ⇨ My number-one StrengthsFinder is Communication.
- ⇨ For the last 25 years, I have communicated with one primary group with only a three-year span (7th-9th graders), typically three times a week.

In other words, throughout my 29 years of youth ministry, I have found my communication process to be different than most. One might say that I'm exceptional, special, weird, or simply a unicorn. Please keep all that in mind as you read about my process.

Our Student Ministry subscribes to the Middle School Curriculum from Orange Students. What an incredible gift to start each week with such a thorough and engaging base of content!

I don't begin my process more than 24 hours before I teach. To start, I open the provided Communicator Guide for that week in the Word document form on my computer. I read it from top to bottom. Occasionally, I use the outline at the beginning of the Communicator Guide, but the majority of the time, I use the full script filled with relevant examples and Scriptural context.

As I work through the script a second time, I:

⇨ delete sections or statements that I find won't resonate with my students.
⇨ add additional Scripture to support the primary Orange verse(s).
⇨ add examples that I know my students are experiencing.
⇨ look for places to do essential "turn and tells."

I am convinced as a communicator to middle school students that if they don't have the opportunity to talk through content, making it their own, they will not remember anything as they leave their time with me.

So, at least three times in my 30-minute teaching, I do a "turn and tell." After communicating a big concept or a bold statement, I will say, "Turn and tell the person next to you . . . someone in authority over you that you have a hard time obeying and why." I then give the students one minute to share with each other. Toward the end of the sharing, I say: "Ten more seconds," and then call their attention back up to the front as I continue to teach.

This activity is so needed and expected by my students that when we have a guest speaker come in who does not allow them to turn and tell, I can physically see them get antsy, as if their thoughts and ideas are about to bubble over if not shared. It's such a core conviction for me that I use "turn and tells" while speaking at camps, retreats, and adult gatherings.

For my teaching time in front of my students, I use the full script provided by Orange, highlighted, not memorized. If I have written my own content, I use more of a bullet point format. I always have notes in front of me.

Our senior and executive pastors memorize their sermons each week. I tried it once and found it to be distracting, not freeing. I have determined that my personality and energy are engaging enough that I can communicate without seeming tied to my script. In other words, the effort it would take to memorize a 30-minute teaching or sermon is not worth the benefit for me.

A few hours before mid-week programming, in my office, I read each word out loud from the script, which secures it in my mind. My script is typically on my computer (with an orange case!), on a high-top table, on the stage. I stand because I am a mover and a shaker—a stool would just get in the way!

The Orange curriculum provides me with a visually pleasing PowerPoint that I can use as is or modify with personal pictures and such—I think I would be crazy not to use it! My husband, by God's grace and kindness to me, is a computer programmer AND one of my volunteer staff . . . so, my slides magically appear in ProPresenter on the screen behind me when I am teaching!

A NOTE FROM

Katie Edwards

JOB	LOCATION	EXPERIENCE
Student Ministries Pastor at Saddleback Church	Lake Forest, CA, USA	28+ years of experience communicating to middle schoolers

Instagram: @katieedwards1212

I love communicating to middle schoolers. They are my very favorite humans to share God's Word with. Not only are they the most forgiving audience, but they are also squirrely sponges who soak up almost every-thing you say. They might not give you their eye contact or you might feel insecure because you think they are not paying attention, but trust me, they catch more than you think. My Senior Pastor has said for years: "If you can preach to middle schoolers, you can preach to anyone." What I have always taken that to mean is if you can take the abstract complexities about Scripture and make it simple, clear, and applicable, then you are awesome. So, basically anyone who communicates to middle schoolers is awesome.

My process for preparing sermons for middle schoolers has evolved over the years, but for the most part, I've kept a core rhythm. I focus on two main things when I am preparing. The first is creating the sermon, and the second is practicing the sermon. The first part is the meat of the process, and the second part helps me connect verbally with what is in my head and heart.

These are the six components of creating my sermon. I might add to this depending on how much studying I need to do or how familiar I am with the Scripture or topic. But for the most part, these elements are always in the mix.

Prayer.
I always start here. I begin every sermon with a conversation with Jesus. It feels important to take the time to surrender anything I am carrying, to

confess anything that might get in the way, to show gratitude for my gifts being used in this space, and to ask for guidance, wisdom, and the words to say. No matter what the circumstances are, I never skip this step.

Sit with the Scripture.
This second step is always just sitting with God's Word for a bit, taking some time to listen and to learn, and listening and gleaning things from God's Word. I like this part of the process because I believe it keeps me from being a robot who just regurgitates information. This time is an opportunity to connect with what I want to teach within my personal relationship with Jesus. I find my belief in what I am communicating and my passion for sharing it with middle schoolers ignites in this part of the process.

Think about my audience and what I hope for them.
This might sound like a weird step, but I like to sit and think about who will be in the room. I let the faces of students travel through my mind and picture talking about the subject matter with them. What questions will they have? Who really needs to hear this? What student am I hoping to share this message with? I find this part of the process helps me connect to the "middle schooler" piece of the communication. And it keeps me from writing a message for old people . . . like high schoolers.

Create an outline.
I begin by putting the bottom line at the top of a document. It acts as a target of sorts for the sermon. The bottom line is basically what I want to communicate in one statement. Then, I write down anything and everything on a document. Following the basic skeleton of an introduction, the key Scripture, one teaching point, one learning point, one application point, and one thought for the week.

> ⇨ The introduction always includes an opening story, an opening of the conversation, and why we are having the conversation.
> ⇨ There is always one main Scripture reference, but there are times when I use a few other supplemental passages. This is also the area where I am thinking through context, culture, and meaning. I spend most of my study time here.
> ⇨ Typically, my talk includes three points: teaching, learning, and application. What am I meant to learn from this, what does this mean for

me, and what do I do with it? Sometimes this varies depending on the subject, but honestly, it's tough to remember more than three things.

⇨ One thought for the week is just the last thing I want to say to them before I close.

Trim down the outline in order to create my teaching outline.
If middle schoolers had an hour-long attention span, I would not need this step. Alas, they do not, but honestly that's okay with me. There is nothing in me that wants to communicate for an hour. So, I take the time to really craft the outline. What are the most important pieces? Does everything point to the bottom line I want students to walk away with? This step is easy. By this point, I really know what I want to say.

I do not write a full script. That has never worked for me. I like a clean teaching outline. It might have some scripted sentences and statements I want to read or get just right, but for the most part, I teach from this outline.

Figure out ways for the main points to stick. (Stories, object lessons, video clips, testimonies, etc.)
When I was a younger youth worker, I used to build messages around stories and illustrations that would teach a passage well. It wasn't bad, but I do think I missed out on a richer process when I did that. So, this is always the last step of the process for me. Taking the time to give students things to connect with that then connects them back to Jesus.

Then, there are only three components for practicing my sermon. Again, this can change depending on specific circumstances, but for the most part, I always do these three things.

1. **Talk it through with someone.** I like to find someone I can sit with and share the sermon with them. Hearing myself say it out loud gives me great insight to where things are unclear or where I might need to add or subtract. It also gives me the opportunity to receive helpful feedback from a trusted source before I finalize things.

2. **Talk it through by myself.** This is just an opportunity to get super-familiar with the outline. I want to know it well enough that I feel comfortable communicating it, but not so well that I sound like a polished robot.

3. **Time the sermon.** I aim for 18 minutes with middle schoolers. I have no idea why. I am sure there are statistics and science around what is best, but for me, 18 minutes has just always felt like a personal sweet spot with my congregation. I have never hit 18 minutes on the dot, but I've gotten so close.

A NOTE FROM

Mikiala Tennie

JOB	LOCATION	EXPERIENCE
Volunteer Youth Leader and Speaker, Church of the Resurrection	Kansas City, KS, USA	17+ years of experience communicating to middle schoolers

Instagram: @mikiala10e

The first thing I do in my prep process is pray for God to speak to me so I know what message I should bring. I ask for wisdom in understanding the Scriptures I am teaching on. Then, I zero in on the bottom line, whether it's given to me or I create it myself. I need the content to hinge on the verse and the main point.

From there, I try to find where I personally relate to the lesson. What have I experienced that would relate? What have other people experienced that can relate? Specifically, what from the age range of a middle schooler relates to the lesson? How can I bridge the gap between myself and my middle school audience? Listening to middle schoolers as often as possible helps me filter my lesson according to where they are.

Then, I look for the heart of the message. Where is there a heart connection? What makes this story real and relatable for someone? Why should they care?

After that, I make an outline using Andy Stanley's "Me, We, God, You, We" strategy from his book, *Communicating for a Change*. I make sure that all the thoughts and ideas I've collected fit that outline for a middle school lesson. I always use the age of the audience as a filter as I outline.

Next, I write a complete manuscript of the talk, including colloquialisms I'll include, jokes I'll tell, and space to identify any object lessons or media I'll use.

With a full manuscript, I can make sure the entirety of the presentation makes sense. A speaking engagement must always be a complete story from beginning, middle, and end.

Using the manuscript, then I create a teaching outline. The goal is to identify the main things I need to say to trigger the memory of anything extra from the manuscript. I could teach using this outline, but it's not ideal because it's usually too wordy to keep track of while teaching. But it will do in a pinch.

The best next step for me is to create an abbreviated outline with simple key words that will pull memories back from the teaching outline and the manuscript. I use multiple highlighter colors (on my word processor) to identify the key words I need to see while teaching that will jog all the memories from the previous outlines. I always highlight Scripture in the same color, so I know that the full context is there and that it's the most important thing.

Scripture is highlighted in blue, the bottom line is orange, things about me are yellow, and general important items are green.

Once I have the outline, I study it until it's time to teach! In general, I learn best by reading, so the most important thing for me to do is read my lesson as many times as I can before I present it.

My process generally works best for people who are comfortable using notes. If I'm teaching on an electronic device, I make sure the notes are in a PDF and the screen is set to stay on always. If I'm teaching from paper, I make sure the notes are printed on one side only so that I can flip the pages and not get confused. I always use page numbers, in case for some reason the notes fall, I know what order they should be in.

A NOTE FROM

Stuart Makinson

JOB	LOCATION	EXPERIENCE
Student Ministry Director at Browns Bridge Church	Cumming, GA, USA	8+ years of experience communicating to middle schoolers

Instagram: @stuartmakinson

Once I have the content I'm communicating, there are three questions that I try to answer each time I prepare a talk for middle school students. I answer them in order.

"Is it true?"

I will make sure that the main point or "bottom line" of what I'm sharing reflects the truth of the Scripture from which I'm teaching. So, I'll read and study the context around the Scripture. I'll spend time praying, asking the Holy Spirit to be the One leading me as I prepare. Once I feel a confidence and peace that the bottom line communicates the truth of Scripture, then we are good to go!!! If not, then I just keep working to make sure what I'm teaching is what the Scripture is actually saying. We're all stewards of the Word, and I desire to carry that weight appropriately.

"Is it helpful?"

Once I'm confident that I'm teaching truth to the students, I want to make sure it's helpful to them! Is it helpful for their stage of life? For what's going on in the world? For what's going in the city we live? For what they are likely navigating in their homes, schools, and neighborhoods? For what they are likely navigating in their hearts and minds? If it's not, then keep working on it!

"Is it engaging?"

Once I know I'm teaching a helpful truth from Scripture, then I can work on making sure the talk is engaging for students! I want to help create an outline that will keep them engaged the whole time, or let's be real, at least have a couple moments that would re-engage the students I lost at some point!! Do I have an engaging story? A good visual? A tension at the beginning that will really have them wanting to know what God has to say about it and how it will help them?

I like to run my talk by a few different people throughout the process. There are great people who think differently than I do and the Holy Spirit lives in them too! So for me, letting other people speak into it always makes it better. I don't want a hundred voices giving input, but I do want a few specific voices that I know are different from mine: a few middle school students, a couple small group leaders, and other middle school staff who think differently than I do!

As I write out my talk (in a Google doc, usually!), I don't fully manuscript it. It's mainly bullet points. I will bold anything I believe is crucial to the talk and is something I'd like to say exactly as I've written it! As I keep reviewing the talk, I refine those bolded points since they will eventually become my teaching slides. I create my teaching slides in ProPresenter once I'm about 90 percent certain what will be on those slides.

When giving my talk, I typically use a "preview monitor" in the back of the room with my "next slide" on it. That way, I can glance at it to be sure I'm following the intended flow of my talk and moving forward to the next point or Scripture. If I'm in a room that doesn't have a preview monitor, then I'll just take an iPad up there that will have my current slide and next slide displayed. So, I'll reference it some, but primarily, I'm trying to stay engaged with the students as much as possible.

This hasn't always been the process! I can definitely recall writing complete talks only to sit and wonder, "Is this actually what the Scripture is teaching?" Or, "Is this actually helpful for these students?" And then having to start back at square one! I may change my process again over time, but for now, I'm going to keep prioritizing the questions: Is it true? Is it helpful? And is it engaging? And pray that God is leading the whole process!

A NOTE FROM

Vivi Diaz

JOB	LOCATION	EXPERIENCE
Next Gen Manager at Sandals Church	Riverside, CA, USA	8+ years of experience communicating to middle schoolers

Instagram: @viviiidiaz

Teaching middle schoolers. It feels like taming a bull sometimes. Sometimes preparing to communicate to middle schoolers feels the same way too. I have a TON of thoughts racing through my head about what to teach per usual. It's a balance of figuring out . . .

What to keep.
What not to keep.
What is a "Vivi preference."
What will make a difference.
What a middle schooler needs developmentally.

That balance is the sweet spot where God uses us to meet a middle schooler where they are, so they can be met with transformation right there too.

My process of preparing to communicate to middle schoolers includes four things:
The Essentials, In Between the Lines, The Tactics, and Trust the Process.

First, The Essentials.
Brain Dump:
This is a necessity for me regardless of what type of message or series I'm teaching. So much of being entrusted to teach is getting out of the way for God to use you. Carving out time and space to quite literally empty my thoughts to be filled with the Spirit is a huge part of my process.

What it looks like:

1. **Blank Page.** (Notebook or iPad is my preference) I'm a BIG fan of no lines. For some reason, I've found that a literal blank page helps with the declutter process.
2. **Focal Point.** I'll write the topic, verse, chapter, big idea—whatever it is that I'm teaching on—at the top of the page to go back to.
3. **Empty.** I get all the ideas out. I'll write down any preliminary thoughts, ideas, or directions.
4. **Finished Product.** It usually looks like this chaotic piece of paper, or several, that doesn't make any sense. It's actually the very thing that helps me make sense.

Pray, Read, Repeat.
While a Brain Dump helps me empty, prayer and reading is my filling process. "What is it that you want to be shared? What truths do specific students need to hear?"

Next, In Between The Lines.
This is where I figure out the One Thing I want a middle schooler to walk away with. After I know the One Thing, I start putting it together. I find myself wanting to teach in a way that feels more conversational. In the first few minutes of the talk, I like to make it interactive as I create a tension while inviting students into the conversation. Next, I'll transition from the tension into what God thinks about it. This is where I'll go back to the One Thing I want them to walk away knowing. From there, I land the plane by inviting them to imagine what life could look like centered on this One Thing.

I've found that this conversational approach with the One Thing focus is that sweet spot that invites students to welcome the change that God wants to do in them.

Once I have my talk ready, I move into the next step: **The Tactics.**

I usually spend one hour of prep time for every minute of teaching, which is no longer than 15 minutes per talk. With middle schoolers, I aim for a shorter time. (This is why prep is so important.) Not shorter because they're not in high school. Shorter because to meet a middle schooler where they are is to consider where they are developmentally.

The three things I focus on in this phase of prep are:

1. **Practice.** A huge form of practice is just talking about my talk. I'll talk about it with my team, with mentors, and even friends. It seals my passion around it—that I really do believe middle schoolers need to hear this. It seals the content. It's not just something memorized, but it is something that I am truly passionate about.

2. **My notes.** This is my outline or manuscript. The introduction and the Scripture are usually in an outline format, and the call to action is typically written out in a manuscript.

3. **My slides.** Having a visual is huge. I prioritize having a picture or a meme more than the actual points. For the points, I'll take time to say, "I want you to write this down." Especially in this digital age, the process of note-taking is not what it used to be. Sometimes students don't know what they're supposed to do with the words on the screen. I really like the concept of showing them how to hear and capture things. Oftentimes, I'll even preface the beginning of a talk with something like, "You have a piece of paper. I want you to look for one thing to write down that resonates with you during the talk."

After I've focused on practicing, my notes, and my slides, the last part is **Trusting the Process**. Like, actually trusting the process. I do believe the Spirit moves the day of, but I've found that it's the prep that really creates the best space for the Spirit to move. The hardest thing that I've learned over the years is being disciplined with both the process and the length of time, which has far less to do with program and more to do with people. How am I stewarding a middle schooler's attention? My influence over them? We can't be wasteful with our influence because we like the sound of our voice.

Truthfully, God has taken me through the rugged process of learning to care more about how middle schoolers are receiving what I am teaching and how they are retaining it rather than how I sound when I am teaching. While I'd love to unpack the Scriptures in detail, or sometimes tell a long story, middle schoolers don't always need that. Actually, it might actually do more harm than good. This type of thinking demands a humility to drop my preference at the door. That is what you call the refining work of God teaching me to care more about the truth being taught and received than how it sounds coming out of my mouth.

A NOTE FROM

Brett Eddy

JOB	LOCATION	EXPERIENCE
Pastor of Student Ministries at Port City Community Church	Wilmington, NC, USA	20+ years of experience communicating to middle schoolers

Instagram: @bretteddy

I love when I have the bottom line of the message a couple of weeks ahead of time, because when I am able to think about them over that time, I begin to see the principle illustrated in people's lives around me—in my own middle school kids or in adults around me. It's like when you convince yourself that you need to have a particular vehicle, and then every time you're driving, all you happen to see is the vehicle you want! I would LOVE a four-door Jeep, and every time I'm obsessing about having one, I feel like every other car I see is a four-door Jeep. It works the same way with a bottom line when you have it weeks before you're giving a message. You start seeing ways that the truth of Scripture plays out in the lives of people around you, building your "why" to share the truth and giving you illustrations of how to help your middle schoolers apply it too.

This is why I love using curriculum (like the amazing curriculum provided by the XP3 team)! I will read through the provided outline and the teaching script multiple times to familiarize myself with the content, bottom line, and main points of the message. The more I have read the script, the more comfortable I am with the topic, and the better I am at integrating the script into my own style, seeing it play out in the world around me, and contextualizing it. As I'm reading the teaching script, I also visualize myself giving the message, listening to my own voice in my head saying the words I'm reading. I think this helps me internalize the message as my own, making it much more natural when it comes time to write my own outline. I am an outline person, not a script person. By the time I get around to giving the talk I've been preparing for, I've thought it through so much that I know how I would build up to, explain, and illustrate the points that I will be making as I build the content to support the bottom line of the message.

Early on in my preparation, after reading the script and before I write my outline, I figure out what type of visual aid I'm going to use to help make the content more concrete. I always strive to have some type of visual aid to drive home either the bottom line, an illustration, or the message. It may be an actual, physical visual aid, a picture in a slide, or bringing a student up to wear a costume and help act out the Scripture, but I'm always looking for ways to incorporate something concrete to help middle schoolers grasp concepts or ideas that are a bit more abstract. Plus, visuals (pictures, videos, props, etc.) are fun and engaging whether you're in middle school or not!

Then, it's time to write my outline. When I create my outline, I use bold text for everything that is going to be on a slide (main points and Scripture) and label my illustrations using italics and highlighting it with yellow, which helps me keep my place as I'm delivering the talk. Using an outline allows me to have much more interaction (visually and verbally) with the audience, which is huge for connecting with middle schoolers!

I usually build my slides while I'm writing my outline too. I LOVE teaching with slides because of how people learn. Some are visual learners, and others are auditory. But I think that you drive home the point even more (and help your audience remember even better) when what you're saying can be read on a screen at the same time. Often, I get great ideas for my message while I'm creating slides and visuals. So my outline influences my slides, but my slides influence my outline as well!

As I prepare, my prayer is that what I'm doing is helpful. I always want what I'm teaching to be helpful to the people who are listening, so as I'm prepping, I'm asking God, "Lord, I pray that what I'm preparing to say, in light of the Gospel and its ramifications on our lives, will be helpful to the students who hear it."

A NOTE FROM

Jessica Hatmaker

JOB	LOCATION	EXPERIENCE
Middle School Phase Editor at Orange	Atlanta, GA, USA	7+ years of experience communicating to middle schoolers

Instagram: @jessicahatmaker

I first started communicating to middle schoolers when I was sixteen years old. My very first talk? I was so excited for the opportunity, but I was also scared to death. I went up there with my entire script and stuck very closely to it.

I learned pretty quickly that, while scripts are great, reading from them as you teach is not. Especially if the goal is to engage and connect with your middle schoolers.

Over the last eight years, I have tried pretty much every method of preparation I can think of so that I could learn what works best for me. Really, I am still learning what works best. I know that how I prep for something like friendship—that I've taught on several times—might look different than preparing to teach a topic that's a bit heavier, like mental health or the sex series.

Some things I've tried have worked great, others have absolutely not worked great at all, and some work best depending on the topic I am teaching.

I have drawn graphic organizers, mapping out my main points and transitions.
I have written out my scripts word-for-word.
I have made bulleted outlines.
I have made creative boards using index cards.
I have started preparing two weeks before a talk.

I have started preparing the night before a talk. (Do not recommend.)

But no matter which method I've used to prepare, I always read the week of content that I am teaching with context for what was coming before me and what would be taught after me. Most of the time, I have prepared using a teaching script from curriculum, and others I have prepared by reading an outline of the content.

One thing I've found helpful when teaching using curriculum is listening to the provided teaching audio or teaching video for that week. Hearing how someone else communicates the content not only helped me get a grasp on the flow of the talk, but it helped me learn and understand HOW to use tone, volume, pacing, etc. as a way to engage middle schoolers. I could hear how someone else was building the tension, what words they emphasized, when they sped up and slowed down, when they let the tension sit for a few seconds. I could hear how they transitioned from building a tension into sharing the truth. I could hear how the tone shifted when giving students a clear step to take after hearing this truth. Now, whenever I am teaching a talk from curriculum with an audio version available, I listen to the talk at least three times while I am driving, walking, or cleaning to get my head around the content.

I am also a very visual person. Or I have a photographic memory—one of the two. But I have figured out that I remember things better when I physically type out what I want to say so that I can see it. Once I've got the words typed, I create my slides, similar to Ashley's prep method. I had never heard of anyone memorizing a talk using slides, but I found, being able to associate a slide with the words I wanted to remember was a helpful tool in memorizing content.

As I begin building my slides, I decide what words, Scripture, pictures, etc. need to be on each of my slides. Then, I transfer what I've written out on my Word doc to the notes section of each slide. I am able to associate what's on the slide the audience will be seeing and what's in the notes section of each slide.

From there, I follow Ashley's prep method (for the most part) when it comes to memorization of slides, transitions, and content. From here, it's practice,

practice, practice. But I am also careful not to over-practice. I can usually tell when I've practiced a part of my talk too much that I start to sound like I've memorized that part. I've learned that over-practicing can sometimes affect a talk just as much as under-preparing. Your middle schoolers want to connect with you as a human, and chances are they will never know you didn't say something exactly like you planned. If anything, it will make you more relatable to them. As an Enneagram 1 and a perfectionist, this is something I have to remind myself of as I prepare for every single talk. I have to intentionally remind myself that it doesn't need to be perfect, and it won't be perfect, but God will still use it. My prayer before each and every talk: that God will give me the exact words that these exact middle schoolers need to hear and give me confidence as I speak them.

A NOTE FROM

Jamal Jones

JOB	LOCATION	EXPERIENCE
Orange Students Curriculum Guide	Richmond, VA, USA	10+ years of experience communicating to middle schoolers

Twitter: @Jamal_Conrad

When it comes to content for middle schoolers, I believe using curriculum that is created specifically with middle schoolers in mind is best. There are many reasons why, but this was the most compelling reason that sold me on this idea: When we are the only writer of our talks for middle schoolers, we end up communicating to them what we need to hear, instead of what our middle schoolers need to hear. This is basically how we are taught in seminary to prepare sermons, which works if you're speaking to a congregation that's also in your life phase (which most seminary graduates end up doing).

The middle school phase is so different from adults that we need help prioritizing what they are going through now in our preparation to teach them. XP3 Middle School is a curriculum that does that for you, so your prep time doesn't have to be spent doing that. I know I am very biased, but I used XP3 Middle School as a youth pastor for years prior to working for Orange.

Once I know the content I'll be communicating, I spend time with the original biblical languages. I personally believe that semantics are everything, and if we want to effectively communicate to middle schoolers, we really need to make sure that we all understand what we mean when we say certain words. I think this is especially important for middle schoolers (Gen Z and Gen Alpha), because I have found that their word world is SO different from mine as a Millennial adult. Almost every week, I'm stumbling across words that mean one thing to me and a completely different thing to my students. So, if there are any key words in the passage or in the topic we'll be discussing, I go to great lengths to find "working definitions" for the talk—definitions that maybe aren't exactly what the textbook would say—but that my middle schoolers will understand to help them move forward in their understanding of God, themselves, and others.

Next, I think quickly through how "Middle School Jamal" would have understood this content. I keep him in the back of my mind as one perspective. Then, I think through how middle schoolers I know in 2022 will understand this content. I usually pick three students I'm close with and who are also diverse in race, gender, socioeconomic status, and family background. When I think through the content with them in mind, I usually find myself thinking things like, "Has Evelyn ever brought this up?" or "Oh, I remember when Tyshawn and I spoke about this last month," "I think I know how this would land well with José." I also make sure that the application steps I am suggesting are practical things that my students can actually do in this context that don't seem overwhelming or unreachable.

I personally like to memorize my sermons, but with a reasonable amount of room for spontaneity. The two ways that I memorize my sermons are by having a clear outline or flow to my talks and then vocalizing them a lot. The sermon flow that I default to is the one outlined in Andy Stanley's book, *Communicating for a Change*, which is a book I refer to on a regular basis. Having a very simple sermon flow makes it easy to be reminded of where I'm at in my talk. When it comes to vocalizing my talks, I memorize them best by listening to myself say it out loud. Ideally, before every talk I have vocalized it from start to finish four times. One of those vocalizations I record using the voice memo app on my phone and listen to that back once. Normally, if I'm able to do that, I have the talk as memorized as I possibly can. In light of that, I try to have as few notes as possible. I prefer to have one page of bullet-pointed notes (what I call my "speaking outline"). I think it makes the best connection between the audience and myself when I only need to glance down at my speaking outline to trigger my mind toward where I need to go next.

Once I have my talk memorized, I begin thinking about making connections with students throughout my talk. Middle schoolers aren't made to (nor will they!) sit and listen quietly for however long my talk is. Leaving room for them to interact with what I'm teaching is something I've done that really has enhanced how they engage with the content.

Throughout my preparation process, I start saying a prayer until the talk is finished. This prayer is related to my interactions with the students. While I'm talking, my mind races with a million additional thoughts, and I'm always asking myself, "Are any of these actually worth sharing?" So, my prayer is this: "Holy Spirit, give me the wisdom to know which thoughts of things to include in this talk from this point forward are authentically from You. Help me to include those things and ignore the rest."

A NOTE FROM

Gina Abbas

JOB	LOCATION	EXPERIENCE
Author and Speaker	Grand Rapids, MI, USA	20+ years of experience communicating to middle schoolers

Instagram: @youthleadergina

I am a youth ministry veteran, and forever ago, when I was being mentored by my Campus Life leader in San Diego, I was taught Ken Davis' SCORRE method.[62] It has stuck with me ever since. It's a method that helps me focus on the bottom line and gives me a format for building my talk. This method allows me to communicate clearly to middle schoolers without being unnecessarily long-winded! In my opinion, shorter talks are more memorable talks.

The first thing I do when I have my content is open up PowerPoint (or ProPresenter) and start making slides. I am a super-visual person, and the process of creating slides helps get the thoughts in my head out onto my computer. I attach notes (presenter notes) to each slide. Even if the slides are super-basic, just a word or Scripture reference helps me get an outline started. If I am using a curriculum, I open the slides first if the curriculum provides them. For me, having teaching slides (have I mentioned visual learner here?) is all I need to cue my memory. Once I see the slide on the screen, I immediately know what I want to say or do while I am speaking.

I enjoy a challenge, so while I am speaking, I game-ify my talks. Here is what I mean: I look for the kid (or leader) who looks the most bored, or falling asleep, or on their phone, and I try my best to see if I can get them engaged. If I get them to look up, lean forward, laugh, or start using their phone to film what is happening up front, I know I am in the middle school zone! But if I don't know my talk, if I haven't prepared well, I am too focused on getting through my talk and not relaxed enough to be really present to the room.

I am embarrassed to admit when I am speaking to my own youth group, with whom I am very comfortable, I hardly ever practice my talks out loud before giving them. However, I do prepare for it well. I know the content and flow of my talk. If I use a curriculum (which we usually do), I listen to the teaching audio or watch the teaching video at least once and read through the script. If I am speaking somewhere unfamiliar or don't feel like I have a good handle on the talk, I practice at least twice. I run through the talk while recording it on my phone's voice memo app and then listen to it at least once.

Throughout my prep process, I pray for God to help me communicate the truth of Scripture faithfully and for the Holy Spirit to prepare the hearts of all who will be in the room (or online) listening to it.

Anyone who has ever done any strength training or followed a training plan to accomplish a big goal quickly learns that practice, repetition, and rest make a huge difference. The more you do something, the more muscle memory you develop. After using the same method over and over, I know what works for me and what doesn't. I also keep middle schoolers and middle school teachers in my life. I know I don't need to be fake or relevant in a flashy way—but I do need to know my audience. Making sure I am not disconnected from real-life middle schoolers and educators helps me to know my audience and makes me a better communicator.

A NOTE FROM

Jean Sohn

JOB	LOCATION	EXPERIENCE
Middle School Director at Gwinnett Church	Atlanta, GA, USA	11+ years of experience communicating to middle schoolers

Instagram: @abluejean

Once I know the direction of the talk, I start by typing out my talk. Someone else taught me this, but I break down my talk into four parts: Connection, Tension, Truth, Application. Once I have all the parts of my talk typed out, I type out how I want to transition from one section to another.

At this point, I prep my talk. Not necessarily word-for-word, but I make sure I know what I need to say at each section. I ask myself, "Can I summarize each part and flow from one part to another?" I memorize my main points, which is usually the problem and the bottom line. I memorize anything that I put on a slide because you never know when technology will not work. And if it is a harder talk, I will voice record myself and listen to it in the car.

I also practice speaking it out loud. I record myself and watch or listen to it back. I notice that when I practice my talks out loud, I find little things that could make my talk better (like taking a longer pause here, act this part out, sit down to show something serious, get quieter/louder, etc.)

And if I am using props for my talk, I make sure to practice with them as I repeat my talk. Does the positioning of the prop make sense? Does it flow with my talk? Can I get to the prop with ease? Does it feel more comfortable on my right or left?

I practice getting through mess-ups and distractions too. This is where it helps to have memorized my main points so I know in the back of my mind what I am working towards in case of any mess-ups. If I can't remember what to say next, I will slowly repeat or emphasize the last thing/point I said so I can gather my thoughts. What point do I need to get to?

Once I feel comfortable with my talk, I take time to rest. I don't stress over it. I don't ruminate on it. I've worked hard, planned, and prepared all that I am able to. I drink lots of water. And I get good sleep the night before.

It took me a while to get to this process that makes sense to me. The most important part of this whole thing for me is to rest. I tend to be a perfectionist, so I will always prepare and have something ready when I need to do a talk. But this can cause me to also stress and worry about it being just right. My brain, body, and soul need to rest. I have noticed that my talks are actually better when I have good rest. I'm more myself, and I have more fun communicating.

A NOTE FROM

Charlie Conder

JOB	LOCATION	EXPERIENCE
Orange Specialist, UMC Youth Pastor, and Traveling Speaker	Atlanta, GA, USA	23+ years of experience communicating to middle schoolers

Instagram: @charlieconder

Once I know the direction of my talk, and after I've spent time learning the context of the Scripture I am teaching, I start off my prep by thinking through ways to make my talk interactive and ways to make it connect with students.

I write out an entire script if I am not using curriculum. I read the entire script out loud the day I write it too. But if I am using curriculum, which I LOVE, it gives me even more space to be creative here. I can spend more time contextualizing the curriculum to my specific students. I think about which parts of the teaching script will really land with them, and what parts I need to change so that it does land. Oftentimes, I will poll students online via text or Snapchat to get a feel for what interactives and examples will work best. I may ask even former students who are grown a question that leads back to the talk I am doing.

Then, once the entire script is finished, I make my slides and add any additional media like pictures and videos I want to use. Don't judge me, but I am super old-school and use PowerPoint to put my slides together! And I highlight the items on the slides in yellow in my script.

Once the slides are made, I leave the slides alone. I'll look at them again the day of, but I know if I keep going back to it, I will change things, which is not always helpful!

At this point, I am focusing on the script. I will bold phrases in my script that I want to say exactly how I wrote it. I highlight the items on the slides in yellow in my script.

Here, I also confirm that any interactive pieces I am using will actually work and not flop. And none of us ever want to flop during a talk. So, if my talk requires a movie clip, I triple-check it for curse words, inappropriate images, and all the things that could possibly lead to a flop. And then, I test that on my husband and my kids, and I even FaceTime my niece too.

One time, I was teaching about Joshua. I wanted to use a clip from Friday Night Lights because no one, and I mean no one, gives a pep talk like Coach Taylor. After watching the clip, both of my kids were like, "Who is that? Is that a TV show?" I was devastated because it was truly the perfect clip. So, I kept it in. I went rogue. And let me tell you: it was a flop. Sure, the clip worked. The leaders all laughed! But only maybe one student in the room actually knew who Coach Taylor was. Total flop.

At this point, I print out my script with all of the highlighted sentences to mark my slides and bold phrases that I want to say word-for-word. I can't memorize a talk word-for-word. So, I spend time in my script. In the week leading up to giving the talk, I read the script out loud a few times too. I let it simmer. I think about it. I pray about it. Oftentimes, I feel the Holy Spirit moving and will switch things up.

If I have to travel to give the talk, I will record myself in the week leading up to the talk on my voice memos. That way, I can play it a few times to myself as I am traveling to get there.

On the day of my talk, I get out my purple marker—yes, always purple. I buy a case at a time. I go through my script with a purple marker making notes, arrows, and underlines of all the things I cannot miss. I don't often use notes but will sometimes have them tucked into my Bible up there with me, so I can quickly glance at them and clearly see the purple notes to keep me on track if needed. So then, and only then, with my notes in the purple marker, do I feel ready to go. I have tried so many things over the years, and I have found that a full script with my purple marker make me the best communicator.

As I am practicing my talk out loud a few times on the day I am speaking, I am asking God that the words I have written be God's words. I ask God to speak through me, to use my voice to lead students to want to know more and love better. If I am at a camp, I am backstage during worship before the talk just talking out loud to God. I put away my script completely and just talk to God. It is a holy moment before I speak. I truly believe that. It is an honor to be trusted to speak to students, and I want to steward myself in a way that it all points back to God.

The truth is, I had no idea how to speak to students when I became a youth pastor. In fact, I had never been to a youth group or camp until I was a youth pastor. I had no preconceived idea of what it was supposed to be like. I just researched and was true to myself. I often get really personal in my talks and share about parts of my own life that were tough. I am careful about how much I share and how I share it to make sure that I am not the victim but to really focus on how Jesus really did change my life. I get so excited when I can share that with students. It never feels like a distant memory. I get emotional talking about how much Jesus means to me, and that authenticity carries over into how I communicate.

Reflect & Contextualize

After reading all of these different ways to prep . . .

What was one thing that stuck out to you?

_____

_____

What themes did you notice?

_____

_____

What are some huge differences you detected?

_____

_____

What is one thing you learned?

_____

_____

What was a new idea?

_____

_____

One thing you want to try?

_____

_____

One thing that has not worked for you in the past and why?

_____

_____

Write out your current prep process step by step
(what you actually do now).

_____

_____

_____

_____

_____

_____

What is a new way you want to try and prepare moving forward?

_____

_____

_____

_____

_____

ENDNOTES

1   "Adolescent Development." MedlinePlus. U.S. National Library of Medicine, n.d. https://medlineplus.gov/ency/article/002003.htm.

2   Joiner, R. and Ivy, K., 2015. *It's Just a Phase—So Don't Miss It: Why Every Life Stage of a Kid Matters and at Least 13 Things Your Church Should Do About It*. 2nd ed. Cumming, Georgia; Orange, p. 94.

3   Arain, Mariam, Maliha Haque, Lina Johal, Puja Mathur, Wynand Nel, Afsha Rais, Ranbir Sandhu, and Sushil Sharma. "Maturation of the Adolescent Brain." National Center for Biotechnology Information, U.S. National Library of Medicine. National Institutes of Health, April 3, 2013. https://www.ncbi.nlm.nih.gov/pmc/articles/PMC3621648/.

4   Brennan, Dan. "Understanding Concrete Thinking at Different Life Stages." WebMD. WebMD, LLC., October 25, 2021. https://www.webmd.com/brain/what-to-know-about-concrete-thinking?sa=d&-source=docs&ust=1642633171797488&usg=aovvaw1elbiamyeysk-bhrotr1-r1.

5   Malik, Fatima, and Raman Marwaha. "Cognitive Development." National Center for Biotechnology Information, U.S. National Library of Medicine. National Institutes of Health, July 31, 2021. https://www.ncbi.nlm.nih.gov/books/NBK537095/&sa=D&source=docs&ust=1642633171793964&usg=AOvVaw2OTX5b04W8zEqjaKCEUkeT/.

6   Oestreicher, Mark, and Scott Rubin. Essay. *Middle School Ministry: A Comprehensive Guide to Working with Early Adolescents*, 70. Grand Rapids, MI: Zondervan, 2009.

7   Zlotnik, Sharon, and Joan Toglia. "Measuring Adolescent Self-Aware-ness and Accuracy Using a Performance-Based Assessment and Parental Report." Frontiers in Public Health. Frontiers Media S.A., February 2, 2018. https://www.ncbi.nlm.nih.gov/pmc/articles/PMC5801478/.

8   Armstrong, Thomas. *The Power of the Adolescent Brain: Strategies for Teaching Middle and High School Students*, 8–9. Alexandria, VA: ASCD, 2021.

9   Jensen, Frances E., and Amy Ellis Nutt. *The Teenage Brain: A Neuro-scientist's Survival Guide to Raising Adolescents and Young Adults*, 80–81. New York, NY: Harper, 2016.

10   Jensen, Frances E., and Amy Ellis Nutt. *The Teenage Brain: A Neuro-scientist's Survival Guide to Raising Adolescents and Young Adults*, 104. New York, NY: Harper, 2016.

11   Arain, Mariam, Maliha Haque, Lina Johal, Puja Mathur, Wynand Nel, Afsha Rais, Ranbir Sandhu, and Sushil Sharma. "Maturation of the Adolescent Brain." National Center for Biotechnology Information, U.S. National Library of Medicine. National Institutes of Health, April 3, 2013. https://www.ncbi.nlm.nih.gov/pmc/articles/PMC3621648/.

12   "3.3 Social Development in Adolescence." Department of Health. Commonwealth of Australia, 2004. https://www1.health.gov.au/inter-net/publications/publishing.nsf/Content/drugtreat-pubs-front2-wk-toc~drugtreat-pubs-front2-wk-secb~drugtreat-pubs-front2-wk-secb-3~drugtreat-pubs-front2-wk-secb-3-3.

13   It's Just a Phase. The reThink Group, Inc. https://justaphase.com/.

14   Joiner, R. and Ivy, K., 2015. *It's Just a Phase—So Don't Miss It: Why Every Life Stage of a Kid Matters and at Least 13 Things Your Church Should Do About It*. 2nd ed. Cumming, Georgia; Orange, p. 43.

15   Arain, Mariam, Maliha Haque, Lina Johal, Puja Mathur, Wynand Nel, Afsha Rais, Ranbir Sandhu, and Sushil Sharma. "Maturation of the Adolescent Brain." National Center for Biotechnology Information, U.S. National Library of Medicine. National Institutes of Health, April 3, 2013. https://www.ncbi.nlm.nih.gov/pmc/articles/PMC3621648/.

16   Oestreicher, Mark, and Scott Rubin. Essay. *Middle School Ministry: A Comprehensive Guide to Working with Early Adolescents*, 75. Grand Rapids, MI: Zondervan, 2009.

17   The Feelings Wheel created by XP3 Middle School.

18   "SF: What Is Sticky Faith?" Fuller Youth Institute. Fuller Youth Institute, https://fulleryouthinstitute.org/stickyfaith.

19   Joiner, R. and Ivy, K., 2015. *It's Just a Phase—So Don't Miss It: Why Every Life Stage of a Kid Matters and at Least 13 Things Your Church Should Do About It.* 2nd ed. Cumming, Georgia; Orange, p. 94.

20   Robbins, Duffy, and Doug Fields. *Speaking to Teenagers: How to Think About, Create, and Deliver Effective Messages*, 109. Grand Rapids, MI: Zondervan, 2007.

21   Advanced Messaging Design and Delivery, The Oratium Master Class.

22   Hemez, Paul, and Chanell Washington. "Percentage and Number of Children Living with Two Parents Has Dropped since 1968." Census. gov. United States Census Bureau, October 8, 2021. https://www. census.gov/library/stories/2021/04/number-of-children-living-only-with-their-mothers-has-doubled-in-past-50-years.html.

23   Hebrews 5:12-14 NLT

24   "English Idioms: EF: United States." EF. Education First LTD. https:// www.ef.edu/english-resources/english-idioms/.

25   "Koine." Encyclopædia Britannica. Encyclopædia Britannica, Inc. https://www.britannica.com/topic/Koine-Greek-language.

26   King James Version

27   New Living Translation

28   Acts 1:8 NIV

29   Acts 1:8 NLT

30   "Hermeneutic Definition & Meaning." Merriam-Webster. Merriam-Webster, Inc., https://www.merriam-webster.com/dictionary/hermeneutic.

31   "Homiletic Definition & Meaning." Merriam-Webster. Merriam-Webster, Inc., https://www.merriam-webster.com/dictionary/homiletic.

32   Sprenger, Marilee. *Becoming A "Wiz" at Brain-Based Teaching: How to Make Every Year Your Best Year*, 31. New York, NY: Skyhorse Publishing, 2015.

33   Talley, Brett. "2021-2022 Scope & Cycle Resources." Orange Students. The reThink Group, August 26, 2021. https://orangestudents.com/scope-cycle-resources/.

34   "Context Definition & Meaning." Merriam-Webster. Merriam-Webster, Inc., https://www.merriam-webster.com/dictionary/context.

35   "Contextualize Definition & Meaning." Merriam-Webster. Merriam-Webster, Inc., https://www.merriam-webster.com/dictionary/contextualize.

36   Advanced Messaging Design and Delivery, The Oratium Master Class.

37   Stanley, Andy, and Lane Jones. *Communicating for a Change: Seven Keys to Irresistible Communication*, 197. Colorado Springs, CO: Multnomah, 2006.

38   Sparks, Sarah D. "Differentiated Instruction: A Primer." Education Week. Editorial Projects in Education, Inc., December 23, 2020. https://www.edweek.org/leadership/differentiated-instruction-a-primer/2015/01.

39   "Learning Styles: Fact or Fiction? What This Decades-Old Theory Can Teach Us." Waterford.org. Waterford.org, October 30, 2019. https://www.waterford.org/education/learning-styles-theory/.

40   King, Alison. "From Sage on the Stage to Guide on the Side." Taylor & Francis, Ltd. https://faculty.washington.edu/kate1/ewExternalFiles/SageOnTheStage.pdf.

41   Brown, Peter C., Henry L. Roediger III, and Mark A. McDaniel. *Make It Stick: The Science of Successful Learning*, 100. Cambridge, MA: The Belknap Press of Harvard University Press, 2018.

42   Joiner, Reggie, and Kristen Ivy. *Playing for Keeps: What You Do This Week Matters*. Cumming, GA: Orange, a division of the reThink Group, Inc., 2013.

43   Novello, Jonathon. "Laughter: Good for Your Brain." Office of the University Physician. Michigan State University, https://health4u.msu.edu/articles/2019-laughter-good-for-your-brain.

44   Boger, Kris. "The Rise of Short-Form Video & The Gen Z Social Revolution." The Rise of Short-Form Video & the Gen Z Social Revolution | IAB UK. IAB, October 20, 2020. https://www.iabuk.com/opinions/rise-short-form-video-gen-z-social-revolution.

45   "YouTube Average Video Length by Category 2018." Statista. Statista, August 23, 2021. https://www.statista.com/statistics/1026923/youtube-video-category-average-length/.

46   Sprenger, Marilee. *Becoming A "Wiz" at Brain-Based Teaching: How to Make Every Year Your Best Year*, 128. New York, NY: Skyhorse Publishing, 2015.

47   Advanced Messaging Design and Delivery, The Oratium Master
     Class.

48   "Lincoln Delivers Gettysburg Address." History. A&E Television Net-
     works, March 10, 2010. https://www.history.com/this-day-in-history/
     lincoln-delivers-gettysburg-address.

49   Johnston, Kurt. *Controlled Chaos: Making Sense of Junior High
     Ministry*, 118–19. San Diego, CA: The Youth Cartel, 2018.

50   Bohinc, Ashley, and Crystal Chiang. *The Art of Group Talk: How to
     Lead Better Conversations with Teenage Girls*, 87. Cumming, GA:
     Orange, 2018.

51   Johnston, Kurt. *Controlled Chaos: Making Sense of Junior High
     Ministry*, 119. San Diego, CA: The Youth Cartel, 2018.

52   Agarwal, Pooja K., and Patrice M. Bain. *Powerful Teaching: Unleash
     the Science of Learning*, 198. San Francisco, CA: Jossey-Bass, 2019.

53   Advanced Messaging Design and Delivery, The Oratium Master
     Class.

54   "The Best Leadership Assessment Tools for You: Jeff Henderson."
     FOR: A Jeff Henderson Company. The FOR Company, August 16,
     2021. https://jeffhenderson.com/assessments/.

55   "How Much of Communication Is Nonverbal?" UTPB. The Universi-
     ty of Texas Permian Basin, November 3, 2020. https://online.utpb.
     edu/about-us/articles/communication/how-much-of-communica-
     tion-is-nonverbal/.

56   Robbins, Duffy, and Doug Fields. *Speaking to Teenagers: How to
     Think About, Create, and Deliver Effective Messages*, 92. Grand
     Rapids, MI: Zondervan, 2007.

57   Wooden, John, and Steve Jamison. *Wooden: A Lifetime of Obser-
     vations and Reflections On and Off the Court*, 63. New York, NY:
     McGraw-Hill, 1997.

58   Adamson, Dave. *MetaChurch: How to Use Digital Ministry to Reach People and Make Disciples*. Cumming, GA. Orange, 2022.

59   Adamson, Dave. *MetaChurch: How to Use Digital Ministry to Reach People and Make Disciples*. Cumming, GA. Orange, 2022.

60   Joiner, R. and Ivy, K., 2015. *It's Just a Phase—So Don't Miss It: Why Every Life Stage of a Kid Matters and at Least 13 Things Your Church Should Do About It*. 2nd ed. Cumming, Georgia; Orange, p. 165, 167.

61   Sprenger, Marilee. *Becoming A "Wiz" at Brain-Based Teaching: How to Make Every Year Your Best Year*, 86. New York, NY: Skyhorse Publishing, 2015.

62   "The Art and Business of Public Speaking." SCORRE Training. SCORRE TM Training, https://www.scorretraining.com/.

MIDDLE SCHOOL
XP3
TRD MRK
STUDENT CURRICULUM

YOU'VE GOT A LOT TO DO.

You need a ministry curriculum
that helps you...

- ☑ Lead great volunteers
- ☑ Engage your students
- ☑ Partner with parents
- ☑ Make your time count
- ☑ Plan your year

AND supports you with a dedicated ministry specialist to
help you make the most of your curriculum and ministry strategy.

Luckily, there's XP3 Middle School—curriculum
designed specifically for 6th through 8th graders.

TRY IT FREE AT THINKORANGE.COM/XP3

MORE FROM ASHLEY BOHINC

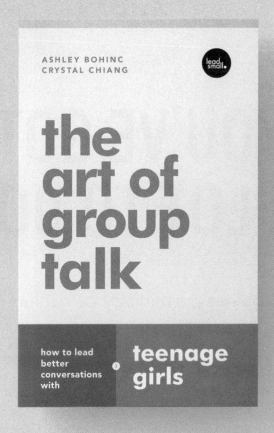

Sometimes teenage girls talk too much. Sometimes they don't talk enough. If you've ever wished you knew what to say or not say, when to talk or listen, or how to get them to talk or listen, this book is for you.

The Art of Group Talk is a 3-part series of books or leaders of kids, teenage girls, and teenage guys.

FIND IT AT ORANGESTORE.ORG